Spience-Bridging Science and Spirit

The quick and easy way to Jumpstart
you out of depression addiction, toxic
relationships low self esteem and into
finding your purpose and authentic self

By
Robyn Wright MSW

BALBOA.
PRESS
A DIVISION OF HAY HOUSE

ISBN: 978-1-4525-4824-1 (sc)
ISBN: 978-1-4525-4823-4 (e)

Balboa Press books may be ordered through booksellers or by contacting:

Balboa Press
A Division of Hay House
1663 Liberty Drive
Bloomington, IN 47403
www.balboapress.com
1-(877) 407-4847

Because of the dynamic nature of the Internet, any web addresses or links contained in this book may have changed since publication and may no longer be valid. The views expressed in this work are solely those of the author and do not necessarily reflect the views of the publisher, and the publisher hereby disclaims any responsibility for them.

The author of this book does not dispense medical advice or prescribe the use of any technique as a form of treatment for physical, emotional, or medical problems without the advice of a physician, either directly or indirectly. The intent of the author is only to offer information of a general nature to help you in your quest for emotional and spiritual well-being. In the event you use any of the information in this book for yourself, which is your constitutional right, the author and the publisher assume no responsibility for your actions.

Any people depicted in stock imagery provided by Thinkstock are models, and such images are being used for illustrative purposes only.
Certain stock imagery © Thinkstock.

Printed in the United States of America

Balboa Press rev. date:3/26/2012

SPIENCE

BRIDGING SCIENCE AND SPIRIT

Develop emotional and mental clarity
Find your purpose and enhance the depth
of your personal goals

Remove addictive behaviors keeping
you from your authentic self

By Robyn Wright MSW

Table of Contents

Introduction

The word *dark* can not capture the complete inability to perceive even a speck of light that occurs during the night in the jungle. It is utterly impossible to see one's own hand even when held one inch from one's face. You are eerily sightless. So when two men violently woke me at 3 a.m. this sense of not being able to see was what I encountered. I did not know or understand who they were or what they wanted. They stealthily climbed in through my kitchen window after inaudibly removing the security bars. They brought with them a baseball bat and used it to beat me mercilessly before I had a chance to wake up. We want to think we are safe in our own homes and I could not even imagine that this was actually happening. I never feared for my safety while I was at my home in Costa Rica. My partner had left to visit family in the United States a few days before the attack, so I was left to my own devices on how to cope with this insane thing happening to me. There was no one to help me and there were no neighbors close enough to hear my screams. It was just me and my attackers. I felt completely vulnerable and defenselessness.

At first I thought it was just a dream because things like this only happen to other people. The intruders had cut my telephone line, somehow broken through the security bars, killed my dog and were now viciously beating me. I thought soon I would wake up and find this is all a horrible nightmare.

Fighting for my life I unexpectedly heard my inner self tell me to stop fighting, stop screaming and go into a deep meditation in three breaths. I did not argue. I did exactly what I was told. I paid attention to my inner self. Paying attention to my inner self during the attack was what led me to survive the ordeal.

After this horrendous event of being beaten and raped and having my beloved dog killed, I used what I know from science and metaphysical studies to help me understand this episode and give me peace. There were lessons in this event for me to learn and use. Finding out what those lessons were assisted me in moving forward in my life without developing the usual symptoms of a traumatic event. No depression, irrational fear, anxiety or post traumatic stress disorder (PTSD).

By looking at this attack with my belief system of "everything happens for a reason" and this was "something I needed to learn from" I had the ability to overcome it with no remorse. Changing the way you view life, changes how you react to life. This is what I want to share with you in this book.

I work as a non traditional therapist helping people who are depressed, addicted to illegal and legal drugs and generally lost as to how to get themselves healthy and happy. The attack gave me the chance to walk my talk. It's one thing to teach others how to live life with no fear - it is another to show how it works in real life situations.

What I find most interesting with my clients is that they have one thing in common: they have all lost their purpose. It does not matter if they come to me for heroin addiction, cocaine addiction, alcoholism, anti-depressant/psychiatric prescription addiction, obesity, health issues, toxic relationships or suicidal thoughts. All of them have lost their purpose for their lives or they have veered off course and need to re align themselves. They each need help in finding a way back to their reason for being. They need a way to allow themselves to find their uniqueness and how to give this gift to their world.

Most people don't pay attention to the voice that we all have inside. This guidance system is called many names by many people. Some call it the spiritual self, angels, god, authentic self or intuition. Whatever name you want to call it, this voice comes from the same place. The communication between self and authentic self has been cut off for many people. As a therapist it is my responsibility to open up that communication line and guide people into ways to listen to this part of themselves. Once a person begins "hearing" this voice, options for solving struggles and challenges appear and an action plan can be developed to face any situation one may find themselves. This does not always make the problem disappear but can make the problem smaller and less daunting.

Many hurting people in the world turn to some type of addiction to self- medicate and numb out when facing challenges that seem unsolvable. There are 18 million adults addicted to alcohol in the United States. Anti-depressant prescriptions total 118 million yearly. Three out of every four people are depressed. This is how so many people of today face problems and issues in their life. They have not learned or have been taught other coping mechanisms. Spience shows us a natural way to cope. A way our body can understand and is intended to understand.

This method of using drugs to cope with stress, pain and anxiety is not how the body heals itself. We have a natural process of healing ourselves and taking a pill or using an artificial method to cope with an unpleasant life situation doesn't solve the problem. This book teaches how to find your inner guidance in a natural way. You will learn how stress in your life causes health issues and how to use your thoughts to "un-stress" yourself.

We now understand more about how our bodies work than even a decade ago. The brain is a big chemical factory and neuroscientists are learning every day how our brains can help us heal naturally by the most powerful tool we have - our thoughts!

There are many books that discuss these principles of science and spirituality. As a therapist, I will show you how to implement these practices into your life with exercises and examples. I not only discuss the philosophy of how your thoughts work, I will also use real life situations to demonstrate the effectiveness of using these methods. This is a how-to book from the perspective of a therapist who uses this understanding successfully in my practice with real people with real problems.

Bridging knowledge from the spiritual realm and scientific research , Spience, puts you on the road to self discovery. Spience shows you why your life isn't going the way you want and what to do about it from the perspective of both the spiritual and scientific worlds. It explains why you keep making the same choices over and over again. You will learn how to make just a few simple changes in your of life to unfasten the ropes that are holding you down. You will transform your life with this expanded awareness and evolve into that person who knows what job they want, how to be healthy and happy, how to have healthy relationships, and what steps to take to get back to your purpose in life!

SPIENCE

What is spience?

It is a new word I created several years ago. I wanted a word that would express a belief system that includes both spirituality and science. The word spience is a combination of these two words. Spirituality and science both have a role in explaining to humankind what this world is, how we are supposed to live a natural, healthy life and what laws govern this dimension. As we evolve, our language certainly needs to follow along.. Our world is expanding rapidly with knowledge and our language needs to reflect these changes as well. New words are put into our culture every year that help define new views and explain who we are and how we now think. Spience is a blending of two different systems of thought reflecting similar outcomes.

If you are a truth seeker looking for answers, you will eventually find that they are being explained by both disciplines. And, I think both have value in their answers: because they are each arriving at similar conclusions. Amazing! Since they both have been enemies for centuries. Now they can almost sit in the same room and not argue. What is causing this reversal of attitudes? Quantum mechanics (Qm). Science is lifting the veil of the unexplained .Quantum mechanics studies sub atomic particles. Qm explains how these small particles interact and behave. We are learning how light is both a wave and a particle. And it is only because of someone observing the light that it will either act like a wave or a particle. It is our observation that changes the behavior. What does that mean for you? It means that we as people have a much more powerful effect on our world and our life. That means that we have more influence in our life our health than we ever thought before. Okay, we don't have all the answers yet, but we are certainly on the road that leads us to the "Theory of Everything."

In my search for answers on how we can take care of ourselves naturally, I found that ancient wisdom and science both have an answer to this. Ancient texts have told people for eons what science is just now telling us. Sacred texts tell us what to do and science provides the mechanics of why it works that way. Science is gradually coming to many of the same conclusions that ancient texts wrote about. Each have answers for us and looking at both will give us a better understanding of what it's really all about. .

The exciting part of living in this rapidly expanding universe is watching science support many of the beliefs from spiritual writings. Take for example what scientists are saying about black holes. Specifically the edge of a black hole called the event horizon. Scientists propose that a person who might come to the event horizon and fall into a black hole would be both dead and alive. How can that be they wondered. How can a person's body disintegrate in the black hole and still be alive? Stephen Hawking, regarded as one of the most brilliant theoretical physicist, has come up with his theory to answer that question. He states that a person who goes into a black hole actually goes to another dimension. This may be new information to the scientific world, but for spiritual people, this is easy to understand. It is commonly believed that the spirit is a separate entity and that this entity never dies. So a person whose body is destroyed will live on in a spiritual dimension .While not all spiritual people agree on where this place is that spirits hang out after death, it is generally understood that it is still *somewhere*. This illustrates how spirituality has known something for years and science is just coming to a similar understanding.

Spience takes on the task of going as deep as we can to understand ourselves better and to understand what laws govern the physical aspects of health and happiness in humans. Let's find out by rising above the myths of religion and on to the facts of what works and what doesn't work. Let's go to the truth that lies in the depth of consciousness by breaking down the barriers that have kept these secrets hidden.

Science and spirituality do their best to explain these unseen mysteries. This invisible force, that some call god, the source, all that is, by metaphysics and subtle energy, dark energy, dark matter by the science world is what we want to know more about. This force can be explained only to a certain level by either discipline. Quantum mechanics and M theory try and explain how this invisible force works Sacred texts like the bible, the Vedas, Qur'an, Tao Te Ching, to name just a few, try to explain this mystery of god. Science and metaphysicians each in their own way are describing the same thing only using different methods and language. Combining knowledge from both fields brings us ways to become more tolerant and inclusive of each other. It is how we can start talking about things we agree with one another. If you are a person that thinks science is the only way to believe, you are now able to find subjects to talk about with a spiritual thinker where you both agree or find some commonality.

It is a way to answer the question of 'are you religious'. Instead of the cliché answer of "no, I am spiritual not religious" you can now say, "I am into Spience."

The common thread throughout human behavior is the search for answers. We look to experts to help us find these answers. We have several camps that attempt to tell us the truth. Two of them are what this book focuses on. The religious/mystical camp and the scientific camp. There are people who believe only in science and are not at all interested in what a sacred text may say. And of course there are spiritual people who do not care whatsoever what science says. By eliminating a discipline altogether we exclude certain truths. What benefit is it to throw information out the window because you don't like where this information came from. Being inclusive in our search for truth is a superior way to find what we are looking for. What I propose is let's discover the places where science and sacred writings intersect. Instead of completely excluding one way of thinking for another, let's open up the dialogue and see where these two agree. It is at this intersection that truth lies. It is at this intersection that we can utilize this knowledge to benefit us and the world we live in.

Traditionally it has been the spiritual people responsible for explaining to us the unobserved, invisible effects surrounding our inner world. Science took the role of explaining all the unknown happenings in our outer world. This worked fine until quantum physics came along Then all of a sudden the invisible forces that the mystics gave answers to, were now becoming known to science as well. These two world views are quickly becoming closer and closer.

This could have only begun to happen in this day and age because our new understandings that science is providing us with. Neuroscientists are just on the frontier of understanding the brain and how it works. Especially exciting is the field of psychoneuroimmunolgy (PNI) which studies the interactions between the nervous and immune systems. PNI incorporates psychology, neuroscience, immunology, physiology, molecular biology, psychiatry, behavioral medicine, endocrinology and infectious diseases. It is the study which demonstrates the connection between the mind and the body. Something that Western medicine has neglected to do and Eastern medicine has always done. Again, here is the intersection of spiritual philosophy and western medicine coming together. Two disciplines that have been opposed now understand the importance of treating the body and mind together as one rather than just treating a symptom.

There are various sacred texts that discuss how to live the healthiest and happiest way possible. Aristotle states that both "intellectual and moral virtues" are the key to a happy life. In the Bhagavad-Gita it is said that happiness is found by living your life with great purpose. Proverbs 14:30 says "a peaceful heart leads to a healthy body". They tell of ways to help us understand how to take care of ourselves spiritually, emotionally and physically. Science also have discussions as well on how we can live longer and healthier. It is understood that the human mind is constituted to make the best out of situations it finds itself in. But people don't know they have this ability, states psychologist professor of psychology Daniel Gilbert. Cognitive behavioral psychologists state that finding even small activities that will provide a person with a sense of enjoyment and achievement will help with happiness in a persons life. It is Bruce Lipton's insight that leads us to a new way of thinking about how our body works. Bruce has a PhD in cellular biology. He shows us that it is not genes and DNA that control our biology, but it is signals from "outside" the cell, including messages emanating from our positive and negative thoughts.

Seeking out truth wherever we find it ought to be the direction to go. So why not look at all of the answers given and sort through them and use the ones that both science and metaphysical writings share similar answers.

Spiritual practices are intended to develop an individual's inner life. Such practices lead to an experience of connectedness with a larger reality, yielding a more comprehensive self with other individuals, our community; nature, the cosmos and the divine realm. You do not have to believe in a god to be spiritual. Spirituality is experienced as a source of inspiration or orientation in life. There are almost as many ways in spirituality to be accomplished as there are people in this world.

The practice of science looks for how the world works using formulas and mathematics and replicable experiments. They too are looking to explain the invisible energy forces at work. In theoretical physics, M-theory is an extension of String theory. Those scientists working on M theory are describing our universe as a Multi-verse. Stating that so far they have found 11 different dimensions using the M-theory formula.

Since not all answers are known to us through science or spirituality we continue to explore areas where truth may be found. The certainty of some spiritual concepts have been true all along. And science is catching up and explaining to us how they are truths. Science is coming full circle, going back to ancient methods of understanding health and how to treat the human as a whole: body, mind and spirit, that were once dismissed as naïve.

As our culture evolves, we look for understanding and ways to connect to our deeper truths and achieve well-being in all areas of our life. Gathering information from magical ancient rituals of shamanism to religions of all types. to the breakthroughs in science is what this book is about. Spience explains why and how an ancient spiritual practice actually works scientifically.

An example lies within the Buddhist saying, "There is no way to happiness, happiness is the way". This means that going around looking for something to make you happy is not the way to be happy. Being happy *is* the way to become happy. Science can now show us this same concept, scientifically. We now know that when you have happy thoughts, our brain makes and floods your body with happy chemicals, technically known as biogenic Amine/endorphin system. You then respond to this pleasant chemical cocktail that your brain made for you. Because of your thoughts, you are happy. It is the chemicals that your brain made when you think happy thoughts that makes you happy. Science explains how an old wise saying from Buddha actually works. Buddhists did not need the scientific explanation, they just knew the principle worked. It is nice to be in an age where we can fully understand why this works. So for those people who are skeptics they can now understand why this ancient principle is a truth. *Being* happy (having happy thoughts) brings you the happiness because of the chemicals that your brain makes.

There may be truth in religious myths and theories, but there are fallacies as well. Sometimes they get it right, sometimes they get it wrong. One major blunder is of course the feud between Galileo and the catholic church. The church was furious with Galileo's' theory contradicting their own position on how the sun revolves around the earth. It wasn't until years later that the Pope apologized for their huge mistake. Egyptians drilled holes in peoples heads to relieve headaches. Ouch! I am glad that this turned out to be a fallacy. There are far too many mistakes that religions and ancient wisdom have made to write about in this book. It is suffice to say that just because they are ancient does not make them the truth.

There are also theories in science that have turned out inaccurate. Isaac Newton's theory about gravity was the truth until Einstein's theory came in to play. Einstein proved that gravity is not a direct force as Newton had imagined, and that speed, force and time are relative, not absolute. Science catches up with physical laws and readjusts beliefs and truths as needed when more information is learned.

Until just a decade or so ago, scientists believed that the brain would begin to deteriorate and no longer adapt to new challenges as we aged. The study of Neuroplasticity has proven that the brain can regenerate new cells until old age. Even though we can rely on many scientific theories and many spiritual theories to be as true as they can be for the moment, there is much more to learn. This book uses information from the spiritual realm and the scientific world that support each other.

Spience takes you on a path of finding answers for ways to achieve health and happiness using the disciplines of spirituality and science. Questions such as what it means to become the person you were meant to be will be discovered. We will look at ways to live your life from your authentic self. How to create the life you want to live. We will look at how scientific studies back up these spiritual practices. Spience will show you how to find that peaceful place that most of us only talk or dream about

This book is not a set of rules to follow, so it is not a religion. You may or may not get rich from reading this book. That is certainly not it's purpose. The purpose it to find your authentic self and to begin living from there. It will also explain why a truth from a spiritual standpoint actually works in your life scientifically.

There are no easy answers or a perfect one- way solution to the complexities of life. There are no hard and fast rules that guarantee that if you do these five things your life will be wonderful. But there is a path. A path using both spiritual wisdom and scientific knowledge to guide us. An outline to allow you to find your own truths. Each of us have many experiences we are here to experience. It is not my intention to show you what you need to experience but healthier ways to react to your experiences.

The importance of this book, is recognizing the fact that finding your authentic self, helps you discover your purpose for being here. Finding your purpose creates health and well being in all areas of your life. Use this book as a guide to find your innate wisdom to free yourself from those limiting beliefs that have kept you from living the life you were born to live.

2

WHAT IS MY PURPOSE

We are each unique human beings. Everyone has a unique gift to bring to the world. This book is going to help you find your uniqueness and show you how to bring this into your world.

You are not just a human being. You are not just an spiritual being. You are both! What exactly does this mean? It means that there is more going on than us just existing as human beings. It means that we have a spirit of some sort and it is with us always. How do I know this? It is only a belief system but let me show you why this might be valid. . Let's look at some strange things that go on that we don't have any plausible answers for. Take for instance your intuition. Haven't you had some experience with psychic premonitions. A knowing about something that you don't know where the information came from but it turned out to be true? I am sure you have thought about someone and pretty soon they called you or contacted you out of the blue. Some people call them coincidences. I do not think they are. Think of the many stories you have heard where people said that they just knew they should go to that party. And sure enough they found someone who they fell in love with. What about dreams that you have had that came true. That gut feeling that you get, where does that come from? If we are just neurons and flesh, does it come from here? There are stories of adults and children that know of a past life and gave facts about that life that turned out to be true when investigated. How is that possible? I am sure you can all recall incidents that happened in your life of this genre that you just can't explain. There are hundreds of articles, scientific and spiritual, that discuss this issue. There is no proof or disproof of a spiritual existence, but there are too many incidents that are known in both spiritual and scientific circles that are unexplainable except by the use of a spiritual explanation.

As we read in chapter one, science stated that when the body is gone, something lives on. What is that something? I call it our energy being. Assuming this explanation is true, that there is something within us that is not destroyed when the body dies, what importance does this information have for you? Well, for one thing it frees you from the drama of life. It expands your knowledge. You begin to understand that this life on earth doesn't have to be taken so seriously. And we have much more input into how we create our own lives than we knew. When you can identify yourself with more than just your name and occupation, little things will not be so irritating. You can now tap into the vast space of unconditional love. Your spiritual being is nothing but pure love. Your life starts to change when you understand that this energy being is there and loves you and will give you answers anytime you want.

After finding out what you are, remember, you are both a spiritual being and human being, the next question is what am I doing here? What is this life all about? And more importantly what is my purpose? We want to know why we are here. Am I suppose to just grow up, find a partner, work, procreate, then die? What meaning does that have? We usually start asking these questions at a time when we are ready to proceed to the next step in our adventure here on earth. This is something that people have tried for centuries to answer, so don't think that I am going to try it here. But I will help you to find ways to make this existence a bit easier by explaining ways to enjoy the trip a bit more.

This questioning process precedes your new phase. You might begin to feel that something needs to change or be done differently when you begin this questioning period in your life. But you do not know what to do. I call this the wandering state. You wander around looking for answers for this unsettling emotion. You look to books, people, different cultures, religions. You think something is missing, but you do not have the faintest idea what ii is. You are not able to shake this feeling. Some give up at this point and think that this is just the way life is for them. They usually stay stuck in this feeling for the rest of their lives. But for the rest of us, we want answers. We want to know what this unsettling feeling of being stuck means and what can we do about it. So we go on a quest. When we do the search is when we find answers. By not looking for answers you resign yourself to not changing anything and your comfort zone becomes your stuckness. By going on an expedition you explore many possibilities and most likely you find what you are looking for.

As a trained psychotherapist, I use to practice traditional therapy but now prefer to do alternative therapy. In traditional therapy we are trained to help a person fix what is "wrong" with them by talking about the problem. Each week you come into the office and talk about the problem. Talking about the problem only reinforces the neuropathways around that problem. Each time you discuss the problem you build a bigger, stronger set of neural networks around the dilemma. Traditional therapists are not trained to treat the person holistically. They are trained to treat a person without acknowledging them as having a spiritual energy. They care for the human side without regards to what is causing the challenge from a spiritual angle. Separating the person from their spirit only puts a band aid on the problem. It is not that I think traditional therapy is ineffective, in many instances it can be quite effective. There are many treatment modalities to treat different people. For me, using alternative methods is a more comprehensive way to find solutions for challenges a person faces. Holistic therapy looks at the whole human being experience by treating all aspects of *being* human and guiding them to their inner knowledge to help with the struggles one encounters on this trip on earth. By guiding a person to look to the real reason or learning they need to find in any given situation, results in being more confident in their life. They no longer think of themselves as a victim but a person on their journey of learning.

One of the big light bulb moments for me came as a result of treating many people in all kinds of predicaments. I found that each client had one thing in common. They did not recognize their purpose. They either lost it or never lived with one or needed to change it once it had run it's course. And sometimes it was just a matter of readjusting or updating their purpose. Even though they came to me initially for help with an illness, an addiction, toxic relationships, phobias or depression, their purpose for living was missing. This insight helped me change my mode of therapy when I realized what the real problem was. I could no longer treat a person in an abusive relationship by delving into their childhood and doing change work there. Change needed to start where they were today by finding strategies to move their life forward. Getting to the heart of the problem consists of opening communication to their spirit and listening to this voice of their spirit. The voice that has always been there.

Carl Jung, the Swiss psychiatrist and founder of analytical psychology believed that illness or depression is of a spiritual malaise. Jung believed that every crisis a person faces after 30 years of age is in one way or another spiritual in nature.

Each and every person that sat across from me in therapy, no matter what problem they faced, no matter how old what economic situation they were in, were lost because their purpose in life was missing. Looking for answers outside of themselves did not alleviate this lost, unfulfilled feeling. Each clients' problem, revolved around not living their reason for being. Most of the time, they did not even know they had veered off track, some never had a track to begin with. To relieve their discomfort, they turn to food, drugs/alcohol, anti-depressants, psychiatric medication, you name it they tried it, they wanted relief. They want the pain to go away.. They were looking for release from feelings of disconnect with their spirit. Their vitality, joy, peace of mind, health and their reason for being had disappeared. They knew something was not right, but had no idea what that might be. Blaming their spouses, parents, job, politics and themselves did not bring their joy back. Nor did it restore their balance in life.

What they needed to do was realign themselves to their inner life. That part of themselves that holds all of their answers. Their connection to their own inner wisdom was severed. Nothing was wrong with them except they were not connected to themselves. This inner voice knows exactly how to heal and how to show us what we have come here to learn and experience.

When we are in pain, whether it is physical or mental, it is our body lovingly telling us to go "inside" and see what needs to change. Our body is the receptor for our thoughts. Our body becomes the barometer on how well we are doing in experiencing this life on earth.

The way to relieve this discomfort for each person, is to help them find their way to their natural state of being. Examining our beliefs is the first step. This uncovers the *how and why* you got to this place of stuckness. Finding out what decisions and beliefs have been the guiding force in your life will tell you where to start the change work. For instance, you might uncover that your parents told you that you are not as smart as your sister. Because of this limiting belief, you did not have the confidence to try out for a better position at work or even apply to college. Maybe that rejection in high school from the cute girl that sat next to you in algebra, made you believe you were not good enough for anyone. So you pick partners that treat you with disrespect. Some negative thoughts happened so long ago, that we do not even realize they have been making the choices for us for most of our life. Exposing the beliefs about yourself, making changes or adjustments, gets you moving in the direction of your authentic self. You become freed from your brainwashing. You become aware that you are a magnificent being, capable of things you were not aware of before.

One of my favorite clients was diagnosed paranoid schizophrenic. Shane had been hospitalized for most of his last 17 years before coming to the clinic. His doctors medicated him with various types of anti-psychotic drugs. Each Doctor tried new methods to "get this patient well". The criteria for well seemed to consist of being compliant and not suicidal. This 38 year old man sitting before me was overweight, had horrible, blotchy red skin and glazed eyes. I met him at the detox clinic where I worked. He came there as a last resort. His family sent him there to find a cure for him. It was their hope that he could be weaned slowly off all of his medications. I have to say that he was a bit eerie looking when I met him for the first time. The medications made him zombie like and his skin condition was scaly and pimply covering most of his body. This was a result of the drugs/medications he was prescribed. He was about 65 pounds overweight.. Talking with him in the beginning was slow going as his speech and thoughts were slowed down by the meds he was on.

The condition I found him in was what his psychiatrists felt was as normal as he could ever be. This is how the psychiatrists wanted to keep him. The medical field felt that this type of an existence was a success for them. This life was how they intended for him to be for the remainder of his days. They felt it was the best that they could offer and that no one should expect anything more. One of his psychiatrist's even threatened his family by telling them that if he went to the holistic clinic vowed never to treat him again.

After spending time with Shane I found him to be one of the kindest, gentlest human beings I ever had the pleasure of meeting. We had therapy sessions 4 or 5 times a week. Through Spience I began to show him who he was, not what he was thinking others thought of him. Shane attempted to kill himself several times in his life because he did not fit in. I only wish there were more people like him on earth. His symptoms before he came to the clinic were so severe that he could not go out in public. He could not even go out to restaurants with family or friends. Going to a mall was terrifying to him. He said he felt everyone was making fun of him and saying horrible things about him. He told me he could hear other peoples' voices even when those people were not in close proximity to him.

As we talked over the next month he began to integrate information he learned to think about himself differently. His brain was re wiring itself to understand new concepts about how to live his life. He started to communicate with his authentic self and learned to appreciate who he was, not what his family or society labeled him as. I told him one day that he was quite unique. He had such a beautiful way of thinking with love and compassion. He laughed when I told him that I thought if he were put in a village somewhere, he would probably be the shaman. He saw and felt things that you and I can not comprehend. He heard things you and I filter out. He was connected to a lot more information than a *normal* person. He was not trained on what to do with all of this information since most therapists and doctors do not understand what to do with it either.

Our society does not like people who are different. Society would rather have others think and behave like everyone else. Being "like everyone" else is not how all humans came to earth to be. No, we certainly do not want people to suffer. By wanting everyone to be "normal" causes great suffering. And their true purpose gets diffused. When Shane tried being the way his family wanted him to be, he lost his purpose. There isn't a lot of room in our society for people who are a bit different. There is fear of differences. I think it is time for us to learn to accept and embrace our differences and allow people to be who they came here to be. It is us who need to change, not people like Shane. We need to not put labels on people. What does society do to people with symptoms like Shane? They put them in locked facilities. Mental straightjackets are used with all the drugs they prescribe. With Shane, they wanted him to quit being who he was and be like the rest of society. He learned to be ashamed of his uniqueness he had come to this earth with. He reacted to what others saw in him. He began to hate himself. They made him an outcast. His humiliation of who he was became enormously painful to him. Shane wanted to be like everyone else and fit in so he allowed what they did to him, thinking that it would please his family and that people would finally accept him. What Shane worked on in therapy was getting him in touch with his authentic self and learning to find his true value.

Wonder if we created a space in our society for people who think differently. A space where they are integrated into society not isolated. How great would it be to accept that people are different and we do not need to force our values on them. We could encourage people to learn to love themselves by showing them love. We do not need to be fearful of someone who is different. This is what bullying in the school is about. Humiliating people who are different. It causes incredible emotional pain and damage. Our children learn from us. If we are showing our dislike to others who are different, we send that message to our kids. Tolerance for those who are not like us raises the level of love in our world. The medical field could use this tolerance and acceptance in their treatment of patients. And they will if and when we send them that message.

Shane stayed at the detox clinic for four months and by the time he left he was vibrant, joyful and off all his medication. He had no symptoms of schizrenia! He lost weight, his skin cleared up because he was no longer on drugs. He also had been eating only healthy organic vegetarian food. His real beauty began to shine. He could have been a model he was good looking inside and out. He was glad to be himself finally.

When he was ready we took a trip to the mall. The fear in his eyes showed as he remembered all of his past heartbreaking incidents endured before. But he went anyway. Eventually he was able to peacefully walk around using his new way of viewing himself. In the beginning I asked him to rate how he was feeling. A ten would mean he wanted to leave immediately, while a one, would mean he is ecstatic and never wants to leave! He never rated the experience a ten nor a one. He started out with an eight but in time calmed himself down to a five. Many people looked at him and he was able to understand that they looked because they saw his uniqueness and attractiveness. When he changed his perception of why they were looking at him his rating went down to a two and a three. He liked the experience. He understood his life differently now and started to accept himself. He was able to do things that he had been fearful of doing for 17 years. He went out to dinner with new with no trepidation and was happy to discuss topics of interest. He was free to be himself. His uniqueness was something he became comfortable with. The mental and emotional pain he had lived with for years was dissolving. People who met him during this time knew they had met someone special and enjoyed his company. Yes, he did think a little differently than most of us, but he accepted it and was no longer ashamed of his individuality.

How do we get so far away from our own guidance system? By not listening to that part of us that has always been there. We tend to get programmed by our family or society very early in life. We don't want to go against something that seems different than what is seen as normal. If your great grandfather all the way down to your father has been a doctor, then it seems natural for you to become one also. Your inner voice might be telling you that your real gift to the world is in being an artist. You might not want the ridicule or hassle of going against the tide of tradition by saying you are not attending medical school, but instead, want to travel to another country and paint. Your family might not understand. So you cave in to the pressure of doing what is expected. You may even think something is wrong with you for not wanting what grandpa wanted. At this point you might decide not to listen to your voice from within and you bury your unique gift to the world in the process.

Going on a search within, helps you understand yourself and brings you to your own exceptionality. When you find your answers, you have the ability to make choices that lead you to the life you were meant to take part in. I am not saying it will be effortless to make changes, but that is where the "work" begins. The life you came here to live and the experiences you came here to have will be yours again by making adjustments. Going on that search brings you to your purpose. We all want a purpose, yet it seems like this all-important unobtainable thing is elusive. This important part of knowing ourselves is not taught to us. How great would it be to have a class of finding your purpose incorporated into our schools. We are given aptitude tests to find a career, but not given any skills in gaining our purpose, they go hand in hand. Let's teach children that it is just as important to use those aptitudes tests to guide them to their purpose as it is to find a job.

Here are some guidelines to use when you begin the search for your purpose. Accept that right now *is* the time to find your purpose in life. It doesn't matter if you are in high school, married, single, rich, poor, retired or a CEO of a major corporation, if you are still breathing, you have a purpose. Finding that purpose may take trial and error, but errors are just steps to learn from. Mistakes are a great way to uncover your purpose because you have the opportunity to find out what you like and don't like. After many "don't likes" and "why do I keep doing the same things over an over again" comes a time where you say to yourself, "No, I don't like teaching math to adults. I like teaching children how to read." You are getting what you don't want, out of the way... Once you remove what is not working, you can make room for what does work for you. When you are excited about something and feel passion towards it, you are on your way.

Believe that you will know when you find it. How will you know? You will feel it in the pit of your stomach. It's something that feels so right that you can't imagine doing anything else. And, you will feel "high" when you're doing it. This "high" feeling may feel a bit strange, and it may even frighten you. Don't be afraid, it's your higher power talking to you, letting you know that you are doing the right thing.

- You know you've found your purpose in life when it doesn't revolve around you. It's not the bigger house or the shiny new car that will make you happy. These are just goals, but they are not a substitute for your purpose in life. Your purpose in life will bring you happiness and true happiness comes from contributing to other people's lives and making a difference for someone else.

EXERCISE 1. LOOKING FOR YOUR PURPOSE 15 QUESTIONS

These questions will help you when looking for your purpose. Buy a notebook to do your "journaling" as you begin your search. It is valuable to keep all of your thoughts and notes in one place. Journaling is a way to inspire yourself and helps you remember your important thoughts and events.

Take time to answer these questions with thoughtfulness.

1. What makes you smile? (Activities, people, events, hobbies, projects, etc.)

2. What were your favorite things to do in the past? What about now?

3. What activities make you lose track of time?

4. What makes you feel great about yourself?

5. Who inspires you most? (Anyone you know or do not know. Family, friends, authors, artists, leaders, etc.) Which qualities inspire you, in each person?

6. What are you naturally good at? (Skills, abilities, gifts etc.)

7. What do people typically ask you for help in?

8. If you had to teach something, what would you teach?

9. What would you regret not fully doing, being or having in your life?

10. You are now 90 years old, sitting on a rocking chair outside your porch; you can feel the spring breeze gently brushing against your face. You are blissful and happy, and are pleased with the wonderful life you've been blessed with. Looking back at your life and all that you've achieved and acquired, all the relationships you've developed; what matters to you most? List them out.

11. What are your deepest values?

12. What were some challenges, difficulties and hardships you've overcome or are in the process of overcoming? How did you do it?

13. What causes do you strongly believe in? Connect with?

14. If you could get a message across to a large group of people. Who would those people be? What would your message be?

15. Given your talents, passions and values. How could you use these resources to serve, to help, to contribute? (to people, beings, causes, organization, environment, planet, etc.)

Here are some more thought provoking questions to help you on your way to discovering your purpose:

EXERCISE 2. 5 MORE QUESTIONS

1. "Who Am I?" What kind of person are you? What's been true of you since you were younger? Write down all the attributes that you can think of that are truly you. List the things you naturally have learned and

developed over the years. You probably take these things for granted, not recognizing them for the special, significant and unique gifts they actually are.

2. "What Do I Love To Do?" What do you absolutely, truly enjoy doing in your professional life? In your personal life? For each answer, consider the gifts that have helped make them possible. Your purpose will involve doing something that you love.

3. "What Experiences In Life Were Really Fulfilling For Me?" Look for the times in your life that were fulfilling for you. These were times when you were just being yourself. Consider, What was it like for me while I was going through it? What was I feeling? What was important, special or meaningful for me? These answers hold the key to what you should be doing with your life.

4. "What Am I Afraid Of?" Once you know what your purpose in life is, what will keep you from living it? Fear is the number one thing that stops people from being who they were meant to be. Do you want to be fulfilled? Then feel the fear, and do it anyway.

5. "How Do I Put My Purpose In Place?" Your life is moving forward whether you are working towards your purpose or not. So, wouldn't it be better to take one action each day that will get you closer to who you were meant to be? It could be as simple as making a phone call, sending an email, or doing some research on the Internet. Your purpose will be realized one step at a time until one day you find that you are living it. And what if you've done all this work and it hasn't come to you yet? It will. We were all put here for a reason. And, if you are determined to find your purpose, it will come your way. When something that strong is in your heart, it's only a matter of time before you discover what it is. The answer is out there; it's just a matter of finding the right question.

Spend some quiet time with these questions. Don't rush yourself. Take whatever time you need. After you answer these questions you will have a good idea about what you want for yourself.

Now is the time to take your vision and create your higher vision of yourself.

Start by envisioning yourself living three years in the future. How do you want to be living? Using the questions above, imagine what you are doing. Where do you see yourself living? What kind of place is it? What do you look like? Have you changed at all? Do you think differently, react differently to life? How do you want to be? Write down what you want in your life. Ask yourself what are you saying to yourself, what are others saying to you. Put in all of your senses when creating and writing down this vision. What do you see, hear, feel, smell. Get as specific as you can. Write this as if you were doing it today.

Example:

"I am living near the ocean in a beautiful cottage in California. I am teaching others about spiritual lessons in life. I am feeling fantastic as I am living my dream. I am wearing a beautiful sundress that I bought when I traveled to India to speak last year. I feel the warmth of the California breeze in summer and I am relaxed and calm. I can hear the seagulls above as I sit on the deck of my house drinking coffee. I am healthy because I eat healthy organic food and I have an exercise routine of yoga and walking on a daily basis. I have friends that I love being with and having over for lunch and dinner. I have just published my second book and it is getting great reviews and helping many people find their inner wisdom. My family lives close by and we are loving and kind with each other. We enjoy each others company. I am at peace with the universe and see it as loving and abundant in all things."

You get the idea. Use what you understand about yourself and what you enjoy from the questions above to add dimension to your future self. Keep reworking it until you are satisfied. This is how I want to see my life three years from now. Stay realistic when you dream this. If you are 60 years old and your vision is to become an Olympic pole vaulter, it's probably not gonna happen. Perhaps, instead you can envision traveling to Africa to be a volunteer to children orphaned from having parents with HIV. Or, it can be as simple as you are living your life with ease, and you are now reacting with love rather than anger in your life. You don't have to make it epic! Just as long as it is how you would really love to see your life in three years. Dream your life into your future and then "act as if" it is happening now. If your vision is you are at peace, then begin to act as if you are at peace now. Begin to see and treat others with this new perspective that you will soon have in your life. Act "as if" you are this **new you.**

Keep this vision visible to you. Print it or write it out and put it in a place where you will see it throughout the day. I recommend framing it. Find a frame that you love, one that represents you. Put this vision in it and place it on your dresser or computer desk. From now on, your words, actions and choices in life are going to be aligned with this **future you.** You are going to be that person you created three years from now. So start to use this new you, right now. Begin to think how this new you will talk, walk and live. What would this future you say to your children when they misbehave? Maybe the old you would yell and lecture. Think what the new you would do or say and begin to incorporate this new thinking in to your present life. Your future you might include you being with that special someone. When you are out in public, how does this future you attract that special someone. What do you have to do differently? Wear different clothes, change your thoughts about being worthy of being loved? You might envision yourself dancing with a new love in your future life, so you can start on that by taking dance lessons now.

If part of your vision is that you are healthy, then every piece of food you choose to put in your mouth will be aligned with health. You will be thinking and doing only healthy things for your body. You will find your local farmers market and buy organic food. You may want to start a garden in your backyard or neighborhood. You will do some form of exercise. Instead of stopping at the fast food burger stand when you are hungry, you will carry healthy snacks. No fried food will touch your lips. You will be cut out all aspartame and msg, processed and synthetic foods You will be reading books and articles geared toward a healthy lifestyle. There are many ways you will begin to change and start walking towards your goal/vision of a healthy you.

If your vision is that you are happy and peaceful, you might need to look at your relationships, ones that are not bringing you happiness and peace. Relationships that are toxic to you will not bring you peace and happiness. You may need to drop out of these toxic contacts or set up boundaries around how they treat you or what they can say to you, to achieve your goal. You will start to attract peaceful and happy people in your life. And people who are not peaceful and happy might not like being around the new you anyway. People like to be around like minded people. If you were complaining and negative before and start to change into a positive optimistic person, your old friends will not be attracted to the new you, unless they begin to change also. They will start dropping out of your life or try to get you to act like them again.

How you interact with others will change. If you were sad or irritable, now you will need to watch what you say. Happy and peaceful things will be your focus when you speak to others. Your children, peers, friends will now hear you as you are seeing yourself in the future. Instead of finding fault with your spouse or boss, you will begin to take full responsibility for all that happens in your life. You will no longer blame people for things that you don't like in your life. You will be able to see how an event is a lesson for you to learn from. This lesson is taking you to the future you.

When you are not able to get tickets to your favorite football game, you will understand that something else is planned for your life and not become upset or angry. When you allow what is happening to happen, your life will take on a different peaceful dimension.

You might see yourself in a higher position at your work. You will begin to seek out what the requirements you need for obtaining that job. There might be classes you need to take. You might need some certifications for a certain position. Do some research to find out what it will take to get that job. You might seek out others to network with who are in the same line of business. Ask them questions on how they got that job. Your thoughts will no longer be centered around "I hate this job" but will begin to be "I love what my new job will be, you will align your thoughts with that wonderful vision of the future you want. By doing these things, you are creating your life's purpose and your future by the choices you are making today. You are becoming the future you.

Your decisions and choices are now going to be all about your goal and the vision of your higher self from this day on. Everything that you think or do will revolve around this future self. Read your future vision as often during the day as you can. Keep this vision of your future self always in your mind and in your physical awareness.

3

OUR GENES ARE NOT OUR DESTINY

We inherit just 50% of our neural networks. There is an entire other 50% that you get from your own learning and experiences. That means you get to determine what the other 50% is for your life. Your family, your friends or society do not determine who you become. It is all up to you. You may start out life with an inherited baseline of how you behave, but this is not your future. This baseline does not dictate your future. It is only half of what you can be. You are responsible for creating your other half the way you want. Your genes are not your destiny. Your thoughts and actions are what create your destiny. You are unique by what you learn and what you experience. It is entirely up to you in how you want your future to be.

That means that you can no longer blame your heredity your parents or your culture for your life. It means that you have to take full and complete responsibility for every aspect of your life; what you learn, how you react and what direction and choices you chose in living your life. No more pity parties for the way you were raised or the experiences you have had. You need to decide what you are going to do for yourself by what you have learned about the way you were raised and the experiences you have had. There are reasons for what has happened to you and now you get to use those reasons for the betterment of yourself. You determine if you want to learn from those experiences or be the victim and lug them around. **It is a choice, your choice.**

Your heredity is only half of the equation of who you are and how you live. Learning is the key to changing and adding on to what your parents gave you. If we are not learning new things, we are not evolving. We become less "adaptable" in our life. Our brain is wired to learn new things. The brain restructures itself in response to input. Our brain loves to learn. It is our self imposed boundaries that keep us from learning. If your parents think that the best way to make a living is to become a teacher like dear old dad, then you might not experience what you came here to do if you follow their guidelines. Learning to pay attention to your own life and what it is saying to you, guides you to what you are meant to do. If you are going to college to become the teacher that others think you should, and you find yourself gravitating to classes about psychology or architecture, you may need to rethink your major. Following your own instincts and intuition helps guide you to your answers.

As we learn, our life begins to take on *our* uniqueness. What we are curious about is what we learn. Each of us has our own blend of curiosity. That is what makes each of us unique. We learn about things that we are attracted to. As we allow our spirit to lead us to new experiences, our life takes on a whole new meaning and adventure.

There will be those whose cells "light up" at the thought of taking a yoga class or backpacking through Latin America. Others might be fascinated by a particular book or movie to help give them new insight. They might not know that they will learn something for their transformation but when you listen and let your spirit lead, you will be following *your* path, your bliss, your reason for being. Take time to listen to what excites you. This is your spirit talking to you. When you keep your life so full and busy, it will make it more difficult to hear your inner guidance. Slow down. Look and listen to what is in your life. Anytime you feel the need to "be busy" by doing something... stop and ask yourself what is it that I am distracting myself from. What is it that I need. Or what am I not wanting to feel at this moment. Spend some time thinking about what you like in your life and what you don't. Spending time thinking about your life gives you a chance to get off the hamster wheel and spend time with your spirit. Take time to breathe. Each time you take a breath, it centers you. It brings you back into focus of who you are and lets your spirit arise to share information with your conscious mind. Give them time to talk to each other.

EXERCISE 3. <u>FOCUS ON YOUR AUTHENTIC SELF</u>

Let's do an exercise to help you practice focusing on the authentic self. Take a moment to not only read this but actually do the exercise. Read through the next paragraph first then come back and do the exercise. It is very simple and doesn't take much energy or thinking to do.

Stop and take a breath.... A long deep slow breath....While doing this relax the muscles in your body and around your eyes..... okay, take one more long, slow, relaxing breath. And just relax and let any thoughts come up. Do not try and focus on any one thought, just allow any and all thoughts to come any way they want. Again keep relaxing and take three more breaths.....

Okay, now that you have done this little experiment answer these questions.

Did you feel the difference of what you felt before you took the breaths? How about after you took your breaths? What were your thoughts? What were you thinking or saying to yourself? Did your "mind chatter" continue? Does it slow down? Are you thinking about all the stuff you have to do, or did you envision something calm and peaceful. Learning to stop and allow your thoughts come up is the beginning steps to learn how to communicate with your higher self. It is time to get in touch with this part of yourself that you have been neglecting for many years. You may not have even been introduced to this part of you yet. Your higher self, authentic self , inner self, or spiritual self or any other word that works for you has been waiting for you to listen.

This part of you holds all of your memories and has only the highest intentions for you. This is the part of you that has no judgment only unconditional love for you and the rest of the world. When you experience intuition or a knowing about something or someone, it is your spiritual self communicating to you. You may say things like "my gut just told me that this person was a not telling me the truth." This is your higher self helping you. Learning to listen to your authentic self just takes practice, not expertise.

This voice is not the one chattering about what you have to do or thinking about things that might go wrong. This voice does not worry about things in the future or the past. It is just always there. You can go here anytime you want. You will only find calmness here. No worries or negative thoughts or feelings of anxiety.

Anxiety has such a grip on people. Anxiety is the constant thoughts that take hold of your mind that do absolutely nothing positive for you. You think that if you "worry" enough about a problem, then you are doing something about it. Well, you are only worrying about something and nothing is being accomplished to find solutions. It is actually a lazy way to trick yourself into thinking you are doing something. Coming here to listen to your authentic voice will relieve you of anxiety. There is no anxiety with the inner self. When you need a break from your worry, come to this place by taking a breath and relaxing into this space.

When you are worried about something or feel sad or mad.... You are not in the now. You are either in the past or the future. Being in the now puts you back into your body. You will not be whirling in your head with all kinds of thoughts You experience peace. You are not tormented by things that might go wrong or thoughts about what "could" happen or what you need to do. This is a healing place, a place of nothingness and relaxation. Having a practice of making time to go to this place will stop you from these negative thoughts. The next time you are upset or worrying all night, ask yourself "where are my thoughts?" I will guarantee that you are thinking about something in your past or something in your future. Gently practice taking some deep breaths and feel the peace flow into your body as you experience only what is going right now. Your body will thank you.

When I first began this practice of bringing my self into my body to be present in the now, I couldn't believe it. I found that most of my thoughts were not in the present. At least 95% of my energy was focused on anything but the now. My first few days and weeks actually, throughout the day I would ask myself where are my thoughts... Each time I asked myself this simple question... the answer was never "I am here now." I found that I was always thinking about something in the future or something that had happened in the past. When I realized my focal point was not in the present moment, I had to stop and pull my thoughts from the future or past and put the focus back into the present. Whew, this was remarkable. I had a hard time believing that my thoughts were never thinking about what was going on at the moment. At first, this process was daunting. Consciously being aware of where my thoughts were became a never ending game for me. My thoughts swirled around outside of me, my job was to find them and deposit them on what was happening at the moment. My monkey mind jumped all over the place. At least 100 times a day.

Collecting the little monkey and bringing him down into now was a continual occupation now. When driving I used each on ramp as a guideline to check in on *where I was*. And , oops, of course my thoughts were on something else other than driving. Being annoyed by an earlier conversation with my supervisor. There I was whirling about a conversation that had already taken place. Not thinking about solutions, only getting upset by what happened. Catching myself not being in the moment, caused me to devise a plan to help me. Taking a breath and slowly breathing it in and out helped me focus. Feeling my hands holding the steering wheel. Noticing the people in the cars driving by me. Were they smiling, singing to a song on the radio, or were they also floating away to the past or present? When at lunch with a friend, I would remember to be there in the moment. I trained my monkey mind to remember to feel what it was like in each moment. Each forkful I picked up to put in my mouth would remind me that I am focused in the present. Since I was rarely ever "present" this is what it took for me to incessantly remind myself to be here in the moment. My brain was being retrained to stay present. It would take a minute or two to settle down and be there. This did not happen over night, it took quite a while to develop this habit before it became normal for me. It astonished me how "un-present" I allowed my life to become-or was I ever present?

Wow! What a revelation to think my life was being lived out by either thinking in the past or the future. As I began teaching this concept to clients they also were not living in the now. A good number of the people in our society are not connected to the now. The people you know and interact with everyday are not living in the now. When you talk to someone, more than likely they are somewhere else in their head and not talking to you by being present. Your boss, teacher, best friend may not be present with you when they are with you. How much more powerful an encounter could be if we learned to be present with all of our energy focused in the now?

Have you noticed that making changes is easy to talk about but difficult to do? Many people do not want to take the time to be responsible for themselves by having to "do something." They would rather take a pill to lower their anxiety or depression. They would rather keep complaining about the problem. It is much easier to go to a doctor and have the them give you permission to not have to "change" something to feel better. "Here, take a pill." is the mantra of today's doctors. Just take a look around you. How many people do you know that are on some type of anti-anxiety or anti-depressant? Doctors are medicating unhappiness. They are prescribing pills rather asking the patient to make changes in their life. It does take patience to do the inner work, so give yourself time to learn a new practice. Being impatient makes people want that instant fix and go running to the doctors office to have that prescription written.

Anti-depressants are the most prescribed drug in the United States. The use of anti- depressants has tripled between the years 1988 - 2000. The rate has risen 58%. The use of psychiatric drugs causes a slew of other symptoms and side effects which are much worse than the original complaint!

Sitting across the room listening to a client talk about her anxiety, I decided to ask her to do something different with those thoughts. I asked her to describe the things she was anxious about. She tearfully told me that one of her fears was that she would be alone for the rest of her life and that she was probably going to have to live in poverty. Her voice became quiet and tearful as she mumbled these words to me.

She as you can tell was living her life in the future. She had taken her emotions to a time that had not even happened yet and then reacted to them as if it had. Her brain was secreting chemicals with these negative, fearful thoughts.

Her body was being flooded with chemicals that created this anxiety in her. Nothing bad had happened to her. It was only her thoughts about something awful that might happen to her. She was sitting in the chair she always sat in, talking, and absolutely nothing harmful was happening to her but her own thoughts. These thoughts of something that *might* happen to her was making her cry and become anxious. Think of the times that you may have also become anxious over something that has not even happened yet and might not ever happen.

Could she reframe her thoughts ? I asked. She wasn't sure. So I helped her by asking her to think about these thoughts....

I will be happy in my future whether I am with someone or not. I will find fulfillment and trust myself to create a life of peace and contentment.

Was she calmer after hearing these words? I wondered out loud. She told me that yes she was but she did not believe any of those statements. "It's not important that you believe them, only that you *think* them," I explained. When thinking the thoughts about trusting the process of life, the brain makes and sends out calming chemicals to the body. It is the act of changing this chemical cocktail from thoughts of "my life is going to be miserable, sad and full of loneliness" to thoughts that produce a soothing chemical. These new thoughts reduces anxiety and assists the body to exist in a natural state. Changing how you think and what you think is safer than a pill, although it might not be as easy in the beginning. It is more effective, safer, natural and more long lasting than drugs.

31

Make small changes in your life by thinking differently. Even by making small changes you will reap big rewards. Make your life less stressful. It is essential to understand that stress creates ill health. If you want your body to heal and function naturally, you have to remove stress from your life. This is especially true if you are ill. You have to get out of the way for your body to heal. There are many ways to do this. One of the most important ways is to make it a point to give yourself time to contemplate nothing stressful. If you can start to add this practice to your daily routine your health will improve. We have such a busy lifestyle these days. We are in the habit of either going somewhere, getting ready to go somewhere, or on the way to somewhere. We have our schedules and calendars full of things to do. We do not make time for ourselves to be still. We do not make time to find out what our inner self might be saying to us when we are this busy. We need to make our interior life a priority. We need to take time to allow our inner guidance to rise to our conscious level. Sitting down to visualize your dreams is as important as getting to that business meeting.

Make it a practice to create times for yourself to just be and allow stillness in your life. Try out various methods that work for you. You can write your thoughts in a journal, have a weekly massage or take a yoga or tai chi class. We all know the benefits of meditation in de-stressing. Meditation is even recommended by doctors to prevent, slow down and control a variety of physical illnesses. The key is to find something you enjoy that challenges you to go deeper and also gives you pleasure. Some people feel guilty taking time to treat themselves. If this is a problem for you change your perception of this by understanding that taking care of yourself contributes to your health and happiness. You will be able to contribute much more to your family, friends and work by finding ways to de-stress. Appreciate that taking care of yourself allows you to better take care of others too. Let's look at some of the many health ailments stress causes.

- Memory problems

- Inability to concentrate

- Poor judgment

- Seeing only the negative

- Anxious or racing thoughts
- Constant worrying
- Moodiness
- Irritability or short temper
- Agitation, inability to relax
- Feeling overwhelmed
- Sense of loneliness and isolation
- Depression or general unhappiness
- Aches and pains
- Diarrhea or constipation
- Nausea, dizziness
- Chest pain, rapid heartbeat
- Loss of sex drive
- Frequent colds
- Eating more or less
- Sleeping too much or too little
- Procrastinating or neglecting responsibilities
- Using alcohol, cigarettes, or drugs to relax
- Nervous habits (e.g. nail biting, pacing)
- Hair falling out
- Acne
- Premature aging
- Diabetes
- Chronic fatigue

- Digestive disorders

- Hypertension

- Arthritis

- Heart disease

- Cancer

Not a pretty picture is it? Stress is a contributing factor for addictions and obesity. Stress can worsen any already unhealthy condition you may have. Diabetes, heart problems, cancer, asthma, headaches, ms and fibromyalgia are all conditions that can be worsened by the effects of stress. Now you can see how important it is that you find ways to lessen the stress in your life.

Without caring for yourself, you become frazzled and unable to make choices from your inner self. Give yourself the gift of slowing down and getting back in touch with your that part of you that knows how to take care of you, your innate wisdom. This is how we walk that balance between the spiritual being and the human being. We take care of our outer being by taking care of our inner being. Learn how to get out of your own way and let the body do what it needs to do to bring your health back into balance. Let your body do what it knows best in keeping you healthy. Getting rid of the stress is vital to your *inner* and *outer* well being. Do this by making time to spend in stillness a priority.

As you develop your inner dialogue by being in stillness your authentic self will start to show. This authentic self shows you your curiosities and leads you to what interests to pursue. Becoming aware of your curiosity leads you to your purpose. Following your instincts and curiosity is the way to live your life with passion and purpose. If you start to wonder what it might be like to go sailing, follow that with an action. Buy a book, join a sailing club, sign up for a beginners sailing class. Be active in your life! I don't mean keep busy, I mean be aware of what you are thinking and what you are curious about, then follow that up with doing something towards that thought or curiosity. Remember, you are on a treasure hunt and a good treasure hunter follows every lead.

You have everything you need to change your life. Since you are not pre destined to be what your parents were, you just have to figure out what interests you. You have the capacity to learn new skills. You are responsible for your life by learning what you need to do to change something if you are not happy with the direction you are moving towards. You can change and learn. You create your life by knowing what you want and directing this want, into an action. Remember, we learn and evolve by doing new things.

An infant learning language hears electrical impulses that we call words. The baby's brain stores these impulses in the brain. The more the baby hears these "impulses" the more neural networks are formed. The sounds are then "recognized" as having meaning and language is formed to communicate these electrical impulses. This is how we learn, by processing new information. The more information we obtain around a certain subject, the more neural pathways and networks are formed.

We are pre-wired for certain traits that we begin to build on when we are children. But, that doesn't mean we can't learn new ways to be and think just because our parents taught us *their* way. When we are learning, we use past memories and prior experiences to create a new concept. If we only rely on what was told to us, we keep using the same neural network. The brain does not form new neural pathways and our choices become hardened. You know people who are not open to new experiences and say that "this is what their momma taught me" or "this is just the way I am." These people become predictable and less adaptable when situations arise. They are usually not the innovators of the world, nor are they leading the way to new solutions or problem solving. There is nothing wrong with this way of being, but there is also no room to evolve as a person.

Then there are those people who become aware. Aware that they have choices. They know that there are other ways to be and think. Once we become awakened to this idea (that there is more than one way to think, do or be) creativity becomes unlocked, and we can begin to design our lives the way we would like. We can begin to nurture ourselves in the way we intended, by listening to our "inner self" rather than only our inherited mode. This creates new neural networks and opens the door to a more imaginative life.

Just think if humans only went by knowledge externally given instead of listening to that inner voice. We might still be living without electricity, air travel, or even still, be living in caves! Those who listen to that inner voice have many times been labeled, eccentric, crazy and whacko, but they are the leaders in this world.

It is those people who decided to bring their uniqueness to the world by not listening to the "official line of consciousness." They went against the norm and not only listened to their inner voice, but acted on it as well. When we "listen" we bring our unique purpose to the world. Live out of your imagination, not your history.

We are in complex times with complex situations that our parents did not face.. Using the same thinking patterns of our parents and grandparents, will not lead us to forge new ways to cope with our life in this century. By remaining with old belief patterns, we might still be thinking that the sun revolves around the earth, that having slaves does not violate human rights, or that war brings peace...oops, we still believe that!

If I stayed within my own families belief system, I would not have gone to college. I started attending college after I was married and had two children. After several years of going to college no one in my family ever brought up the subject. My mother never talked about my "education". I decided to ask her one day, why she avoided the subject. I asked her why she never asked me anything about me going to school. She looked at me like I was an alien. "I don't understand why you would even go to college, Robyn, you already have a husband." This was my mothers' belief system; women only go to college when they are looking for a man. It mystified the entire family I guess. That is why they couldn't bring it up in conversation. They didn't understand me wanting an education, so they just left the subject alone. They did not know what to say to me, so they said nothing. Hoping perhaps, that I would finally come to my senses and go back to what they felt was normal, being a wife and mother.

I stepped out of my family's comfort zone and traveled on my own adventure. Finding answers for ourselves and looking at things with new eyes will lead you to yourself. If you are looking to transform your life be open to new ways of thinking. If you want something in your life to change; change something in your life! It is up to you to find your answers. **Every answer to every question is inside you.** Take the time to ponder and dream and find those answers.

Einstein knew the value of new thinking when he said "curiosity is more important than knowledge. Knowledge is limited, imagination encircles the world."

Being curious about new ways of living will lift you out of your boundaries. It will evolve and transform you. Only when you can get beyond your genetic thinking, will you be able to follow your spirit and discover why you are here and what you are to do.

Start the transformation in your life by becoming curious about how you got there. Ask your self questions: **What thoughts brought you to this point in your life? How does your family, society, or peers beliefs influence your own. What events in your life were meaningful?**

How do we learn new ways to be and think? By learning about ourselves and understanding why we do what we do. Know you have many, many more options than you thought you had. Become awakened to the power of your thoughts!

<blockquote>

To study others you become wise
To study yourself
you become enlightened!

</blockquote>

4

CHANGE YOUR THOUGHTS

We have 64,000 thoughts per day. Here is the interesting statistic, 95% of those thoughts are the same things we thought about yesterday and the day before that. These are the same thoughts you will be thinking about tomorrow and the next day and the day after that. As you can see not much new information is being thought about. We become strongly attached to "our" way of thinking as we repeat these same thoughts day after day.

With each thought we have a chemical is made by our brain. Every thought has a corresponding chemical for each thought. By thinking these same thoughts every day our body receives the same chemicals each day. Our bodies begin to crave these same thoughts that is producing these same chemicals. We literally become addicted to our thoughts. We begin to allow our body to rule our mind. Rather than our mind ruling our body. This explains why happy people generally are happy most of the time and sad people are generally sad most of the time. People thinking happy thoughts are thinking these thoughts 95% of the time. The same goes with sad thoughts. Depressed people are thinking sad thoughts 95% of the time. They are drenching their body with the corresponding chemicals that they are thinking.

My neighbor is always worried about something. If he has nothing to worry about he will worry about my stuff or something he saw on the news that day. He just has to worry. Worrying has become a natural state for him. If he did not worry he would not feel normal. His thoughts create a worrying chemical that flows through his body all day and most of the night. His body has been receiving this chemical cocktail for years now. If he were to find something to make him happy his body would not like that. His body would find a way to make him worry. He would create some type of scenario to get his mind back to the job of worrying. This is why he likes to watch movies that cause stress and anxiety. When he watches these types of movies, his brain makes an anxiety drug for his body. He might think he is relaxing, but his body knows differently. When the bad guy in the movie is chasing the innocent woman through the house with a knife, his body is soaking up the anxious/worry chemicals to keep his normal state of worry in tact.

You feel sad about the breakup with your loved one. Your body makes the "sad" chemical. The "sad" chemical brings other sad thoughts into your awareness. You think about all the times you have been hurt by loved ones. This brings on more "sad" chemicals. Your body is literally receiving an overdose of these chemicals. And then if someone comes along and tells you not to feel sad, your brain knows that it would like to stop thinking obsessively about the sadness, but your body is so accustomed to having that sad chemical, it has become normal feeling for you. Since 95% of your thinking is about sadness, this is what feels normal for you. This is the drug that your body is addicted to. You are an addict to your thoughts.

If you happen to have a happy thought in there, it is not enough to change the chemical makeup. Your body rejects that happy thought and begs for the sad chemicals it has become use to. You are in a loop that you do not understand how to get out of. Your addiction to your thoughts are ruling your life. Until you understand what is going on it is difficult to change these patterns of thinking.

If you don't become aware of how you are choosing what to put in your life, nothing will change. People behave like addicts, wanting only the drug/chemical, that makes them feel the way they have come to know as normal. We then come to the conclusion that there is only one way to think, be or behave. Your life becomes limited and you may feel hopeless and trapped. Our addiction to our same thoughts, controls us. We are not open to new thoughts. We begin to feel "caught" in our lives and cut off from our divine source. We loose our purpose and the reason we came to be here in this life. Our sparkle fades.....

We are creators, we must create! Human beings are here to be creators- by creating, we learn. When we only activate the circuits in our brain that were handed down to us, we do not evolve. When we only think the thoughts that we are addicted to we do not evolve. We have to add to our neural network by learning new things and choosing different options other than what family or society has taught us, or what we have become so use to thinking.

Just having those same old 64,000 thoughts each day makes you stagnate and less imaginative. The world becomes flat, we get sick and we look for drugs, alcohol or diversions for our life, thinking it will bring us back to some kind of balance. Being unbalanced we are unaligned to our divine self and our purpose for being here. We each chose to be here in this life to learn many things, have many experiences and to feel many feelings. By only activating the neural networks that we inherited, we deaden ourselves to our spiritual life and are not choosing from our spiritual side. We robotically choose from memory.

We have the option to come from memory (ego) or inspiration (spirit) when making a decision or when communicating. When you only choose from memory, you are not experiencing a life full of spiritual guidance. This is where you will find yourself repeating certain patterns in your life, or you may find yourself in a rut. If you have a belief system that says you must always plan ahead and not be spontaneous, you could be missing out on some life changing opportunities. Go with your gut- Your gut will guide you to your authentic life. Say what your gut tells you to, not what you think the other person wants to hear. Follow your intuition rather than your routine memory. There are so many missed opportunities by saying no to a spontaneous invitation for a trip, talking to a stranger, or signing up for a class that sparks your interest. These "missed opportunities" will lead you to your spiritual destination. Just choosing from habit, or what feels safe, puts a mental straightjacket on you. Joy is strangled because you are only choosing what you know and what you have "always" done.

I don't want you to think your ego is bad for you. It is your friend. It has been there since day one in this existence. It has helped you out in many instances in your life. It has a place in your life. So, I do not subscribe to the thinking that you need to get rid of your ego, you just have to know when it is talking.

As you become "awakened" to the fact that you also have a spirit to help guide you, then you choose how you want to proceed knowing your options. Before this understanding came to be known to you, your only alternative was to listen to your ego. Now you have the ability to live a more spiritual life by listening to that voice that has always been there waiting to be heard. This brings you more understanding as to why things happen in the world and how you can react differently to what happens to you.

Remember that you can chose from your spiritual side. When you do, life becomes more meaningful. You will be led to your next phase in your life where you will learn something to move you on your journey. Think of it like a treasure hunt as you follow your spirit. When you look for a treasure you look for clues to discover it. Look for your clues as they come to you in dreams, inspirations and curiosity. It is exciting when you discover that treasure is there just for you. But you have to go out and look for it. When you are given a choice, ask your spirit which direction it would have you go in. After you ask your question to your spirit, the very first thing that comes to your mind, is your spirit talking to you. The minute you start thinking about the answer you are no longer listening to spirit. That is your ego choosing for you. Ego will tell you things like, you better not take the long route home, even when your spirit is imploring you to explore a different road that may take longer to get home. The long route is full of beautiful trees and fields. Your spirit may need you to be in touch with that so you can be inspired. Your ego takes over by telling you the normal way home is best and you do not want to be late in watching the evening news program, like you always do. It takes time to know which is talking, your gut (spirit/intuition) or your memory (ego). Keep practicing if you want to become better at listening for your authentic voice. Be adventurous and curious as you learn to listen to your spirit.

You can do what you always have done or you can listen to your inner voice. It is freely your choice to go in either direction. Neither one is right or wrong. But, if you want to live a spiritual life, you will want to listen to your spiritual voice. You are no longer a slave to your automatic response. Your boundaries open up. These boundaries are what you have put on yourself. This means that you can take those limitations off. Free people choose their course, slaves do not. Overcome your slavery to your repetitive thoughts and free yourself by knowing you have choices.

You do not have to always react with those "same" thoughts. If you lose a relationship, job or have an accident, you do not have to feel unlovable, worthless or clumsy. You will begin to understand that there is <u>ALWAYS</u> something to learn from each and every event in your life. And if you do not take the time to learn what you were suppose to have learned, guess what? You will get another opportunity to learn it.

Wouldn't it be better to learn a lesson the first time and not have to repeat the lesson over and over? Listen to your spirit and hear what it has to tell you about what you need to learn by having that event in your life.

Watch for repeated patterns in your life. They are telling you that you are not paying attention to a lesson.

- Do you keep picking the same toxic relationships over and over?

- Is your bank account constantly overdrawn?

- Are you using drugs, food alcohol to take away a certain feeling, even when you do not want to?

- Do you find that you are arguing with others on a constant basis?

- Are you wondering why you keep losing friends.

- Are you always late?

- Are you in another job that you hate?

Be on the look out for your patterns that you do not like.

Something that I did not pay attention to for over a year was when I began hating my job. I did not take time to understand what this meant. I soon fell into depression. My job of 15 years became unbearable. I loved going to work. I woke each morning excited about what the day would bring. For fourteen years, I loved my job, but that last year I began feeling unhappy, very unhappy. The job changed. Or had I changed? It became less fulfilling and more demanding. I worked as a social worker for a county agency that investigated child abuse. I thought I would stay in that job until I retired or died. I did not know anything else I could do for a living or that I wanted to do. I was afraid of not knowing what else I would or could do to make a living. Do you see the boundary I created for myself? I thought that I had no skills to offer to a job market. I had fenced myself in by my limited thinking that I could not do anything else or that I would not like anything else.

I finally became concerned when I found myself crying all the way to work on the 45 minute drive. I began leaving work early. I complained incessantly to co workers and friends about how much I hated my job and how sad I was. I guess I thought that would help change things if I complained enough. People irritated me, everything irritated me. I argued with everyone including my supervisor, the court, my peers even the car in front of me driving slower than I wanted to go. Everyone else was to blame for my unhappiness. If I could just fix them, then maybe I would feel better. If someone felt sorry for me, maybe they could wave a magic wand and I would be "fixed" to continue my life in happiness. I turned into an unstable mess and not much fun to be around. I couldn't stand me so I am sure no one else could either.

What did I do? Did I think about options to change my life. Did I start looking into my inner self for answers? Nope, I kept working. I didn't even know I had an inner self. I was confident and I thought I could *power* through this difficult time and get my self back to that happy place. Well, it didn't work. I was still miserable and sad and I continued crying the entire way to work. I could not find my "happy." It became so unbearable for me that I eventually had to take a stress leave. During the stress leave, I traveled a bit. Maybe if I just got away for awhile and changed my surroundings I would get better I told myself. When I came back to work, the same miserable feelings gripped me once again.

So, what did I do then? I did what so many of us do. I went to the doctor and asked for help in relieving these unbearable feelings. The doctor was kind and caring. He had empathy for my situation. So, he gave me a prescription for an anti-depressant. This is a scenario that is repeated thousands of times a day in our world. We go to a doctor to find out what is wrong with us, we think they have the magic answer for us in a pill.

I didn't understand at the time that my body was trying to get my attention to tell me something. I did not know that I could ask the question to my spirit on which direction I could take with this problem of depression. So, I took my magic pill daily and became numb to my spirit and the feelings that were trying to tell me something.

After about 3 months, I felt better. I no longer dreaded going to work. I quit crying and kept working. Phew, what a relief- I was fixed! So I quit taking the pill, thinking the depression was gone. I thought my normal happy self would take over now.

Wrong. The sadness came back. My body was again trying to get my attention. It wanted me to go inside and listen. Finally I did just that. I took time to understand that I needed to change something. I didn't know what I needed to change, but I knew I did not want to go on like this. I went on a quest to find answers for me. I went away for the weekend on a retreat to learn how to meditate. I read tons of spiritual books. I took up yoga. I wanted to find the truth to what was happening to me. And I found that pills were not the answer for me.

During this journey for truth, someone I barely knew, invited me to go to Costa Rica and live in the middle of the jungle on 500 acres of rainforest without electricity, cell phones or internet. That meant no hot water for showers, yikes. He explained that the cabin had no walls. The birds, snakes and insects could freely come and go through the house. Was this what I was suppose to do? I wondered if I was indeed crazy for even contemplating this radical change in my life. My body, mind and spirit all told me to do it. With every cell in my being, I knew this was what I wanted to do. So I said yes. I listened to my inner guide and followed it by making this decision to move to another country. I did this even knowing that 1 I did not know the language of my new country I would now live. The word for hello in Spanish was not even in my vocabulary when I moved to Costa Rica. I felt no fear, only exhilaration as I thought about living my new life.

I let go of my old belief system of having to have a house, a job and living like everyone else. I sold my house, quit my job and moved. Friends and family thought I had finally cracked and was making the biggest mistake in my life. I am sure they thought I should get back on those *happy pills* and pull myself together.

Moving to this next adventure was the greatest thing I could have done for myself. I loved every second of my new life. I spent hours doing yoga, reading, hiking down to the beach. I watched the white face monkeys and the spider monkeys travel in the forest that was just inches from my cabin. The incredible wildlife that was all around me stirred a new passion within me. I was living naturally. I awoke to the loud screeching of the macaws as they left their roosts for the day. The howler monkeys roaring so loud in the dawn that I could not hear my partner next to me. No alarm clocks needed here. I sipped my coffee on the big wooden front steps as the sun rays glistened on the forest trees in the early rising of the new day. This was how a jungle awoke each morning. This is how I awoke each morning, in tune with nature.

Falling asleep to the howlers settling down for the night with their howls, letting the other troops know where they were, was nothing less than electrifying for me. There was a nightly show of lightening bugs in the dry season, blinking on and off in my front yard. This was better than any nature show on television. I spent hours and hours getting to know myself in this beautiful nature wonderland. I was happy again!

I look back on making that amazing decision from "spirit". Wow! What a magnificent decision maker my spirit is. I am actually glad I had the depression. I have never regretted the decision to move my life into the next phase. It was one of the most wonderful things that has happened to me. My life was a fantasy fulfilled and I was able to take time to connect to my spirit.

I know that if I had not changed something in my life by listening to what my body wanted me to know…(that it had something better in mind for me) I would have ended up with some illness, extremely depressed and working at a job I hated that was unfulfilling, until the day I died. I had a choice of a bleak outcome by staying in my rut, or going with my gut to live an entirely different life. I chose to follow my instincts and am so grateful that I did.

I could not have even thought about a solution like moving to the jungle, if I limited myself to listening only to my ego. I would not have chosen this wonderful life-changing move had I not experienced the devastating depression. So, when you think something in your life is dreadful, it could be an opportunity to listen to your inner self to make a fantastic change.

The spirit will keep on trying to get your attention. Listen to it. There are amazing opportunities out there, if you only listen.

As you begin to listen to your spirit pay very close attention to what self talk you listen to. Watch what you say to yourself. What self-defeating words do you use. Words like *can't, should* and *try* are useless words. These are not power words. Remember, your thoughts become your destiny. If you keep telling yourself, you can't get out of debt, then I will guarantee you, you won't get yourself out of debt. If you say you will "try" to eat healthier food. Then chances are that you will only "try" and not *do*. You either do it or you don't. There is no in between. These are very weak useless words. Throw them out of your vocabulary, you do not need them anymore.

When changing something in your life pick a *towards goal* rather than an *away from* goal. If you are wanting to lose weight or quit smoking, use words to say what you want, not what you don't want.

<u>Instead of saying,</u>

I don't want to smoke anymore.
I don't want to be poor.
I don't want to be in a toxic relationship.
I don't want to be in this boring dead-end job.
I don't want to be fat.

<u>Say instead</u>

I want health
I want abundance
I want a fulfilling relationship
I want a job that is challenging that has limitless opportunities to excel
I want a healthy body

Change your perspective and your language.
Then begin stating your wants in the positive <u>and</u> in the now. State what your desires are *as if* they are already in your life.
My health is perfect in every way
I enjoy my healthy life
I have the things in my life that make it abundant
My relationships are peaceful and happy
My job I aspire to is fulfilling and makes me happy
My body is healthy and fit
Money flows easily and effortlessly to me
The only limits you put on your life are those you set yourself. Push beyond your limits and unlock mental reserves you thought you never had.

- **Push yourself daily**

- **Do things you fear**

- *Be* **the person you dream of being**

5

EVERY THOUGHT YOU HAVE IS CREATING YOUR FUTURE

Each and every situation is neutral. It is only *YOUR* perspective that changes it to a positive or a negative. You can change any situation into something positive by perceiving it differently.

Let's say you get fired unexpectedly from your job. That might seem like a pretty devastating event. But you can also look at it in a positive way. You can think, "wow, now I am free to go back to school," or "this might be a time to relocate to that new city I want to live in." You can do this with any situation you have. You will be able to find ways to see positive in any situation that comes your way.

This way of thinking opens you up to a lot of power you didn't even realize you had. You have the option to feel sorry for yourself or gain insight into yourself. This allows a lot more freedom for you.

That is not to say that you are not suppose to ever have sad feelings or compassion for a situation. These are human emotions and we have them to express and experience. There is no need to repress these feelings as they will only come up in another way by having an illness or having anxiety or depression. You have heard the saying "if you resist, it will persist". I am not advocating that we walk around only allowing happy, upbeat thoughts into our life. There are very sad things that happen in life. Tragic events are a part of life. Working your way through an event that brings sorrow and grief is healthier than repressing those feelings. Feel the emotion that is coming up for you. Allow it, honor it and release it by finding a way to perceive it differently. Is there something you can learn from this event? Seeing what there is to learn from the event helps you to deal with it. Holding on to negative emotions causes health problems. Learning what to do with those emotions is what is important. Ask your inner guidance what are you suppose to understand about the situation, and your healing process begins.

Now you have a wider range of how you want to express yourself. You do not have to come from your automatic response of seeing only the negative. You can now go directly to your spirit and find answers and directions on how to proceed when you look for that learning/lesson. Think of it as an opportunity that will help you evolve and transform your life.

Next time you can't find your keys and this causes you to be late for an appointment, instead of being anxious and upset, find a way to understand how this could be positive. Maybe you will get that perfect parking space right by the entrance. Maybe you will have missed a traffic jam or even an accident by being late.

Do you have a boring job, an unfulfilling relationship, do you get sick often or find yourself always out of money? You are not going to change any of these things by thinking the same thoughts of how awful this is. You need to check to see what this situation is wanting to teach you. Maybe you need to hate your job so you will find a better one. The same with being broke, it can lead you into researching new ways of making a living more suitable for your purpose. Or you may decide to downsize by moving to a smaller more affordable home. A simple lifestyle could mean less stress that is needed in your life. Change your perspective on your challenges in life and see them as opportunities and a way to move forward on your journey. To change something, anything, in your life, you have to change your thoughts about it.

It is **_imperative_** to find your belief system about something that you want to change. Discovering a limiting belief helps you understand why you make certain choices that do not make sense to you or anyone else. You might find out that the reason you always give in to your partner comes from an irrational fear you carry from your past. Your parent might have humiliated you to get you to clean up the house or take out the trash. Your belief might be that if you do not do what you are told to do, you are going to be inflicted with emotional pain. Becoming the peacemaker was your way to lessen your fear of being shamed. You take on the task of always doing what someone wants you to do, even at the risk of you losing your individuality. Being in fear of that terrible feeling dictates how you act and react. That fear becomes more important than feeling good about yourself. Avoiding that feeling becomes paramount. Your decisions become based on this limiting irrational belief of fear. After years of behaving this way, you just figure this is how you are and do not question it.

Finding that fear and changing how you react to it changes your life. Discovering your hidden beliefs allows you to make choices that you did not know you had. Your authentic voice is found outside of all of your programming. Confidence is found here. Curiosity comes from here. Many options and opportunities open up.. Being aware of hidden fears allows abilities to be unleashed. Instead of always doing what someone wants you to do, find instead, what your spirit is wanting for you. Following your own path is empowering. Revealing your belief system rids irrational beliefs that keep you stuck. You can't change what you don't know is there. That is why the search for those limiting beliefs is so important.

If you want to change your financial situation, understand thoughts about money. What did your parents think about money when growing up. Were they always poor? Did they believe in saving money, did they spend more than they earned. Delve into how you came to your beliefs about what ever you want to change.

If you want a better relationship, ask your self what your beliefs are about healthy relationships. Did your parents have a healthy relationship. Did they fight, have little communication with each other, did they enjoy each others company? Ask yourself questions about where your belief really stems from.

If you are sick and want better health, uncover your belief system about what is health to you. How did you grow up thinking about being healthy. Did your parents take you to the doctors constantly? Did they worry about their own health persistently. Did you get attention by being sick? Was health not a priority for your family? Find out where you got your thoughts. You will have to change your thoughts about what it is that you want different in your life. To do that, you will need to know what thoughts need changing. Investigate by asking yourself questions to see what thought keep you creating the situation.

When you find yourself in reoccurring patterns, the universe is giving you an opportunity to learn something from it. If you don't learn it, then guess what? Yep, the universe will give you another opportunity by having this pattern repeat itself in your life. So, won't it be better to learn it now?

EXERCISE 4. <u>CHANGING YOUR BELIEFS</u>

Ok, so let's see what is required to go on a hunt for those repressed beliefs. How *do* we find our belief system? Good question. And there are numerous ways to go about this very important task. Here is one way that has helped many of my clients.

First of all pick a word or belief that you want to find more about. A word or a belief that you want to see where your ideas around it came from. For instance take the word LOVE…. Lots of different ways to view that word. All of us have our own way we think about it. Let's take a look and see what your belief system is, about love.

Write the word *love* at the top of a piece of paper. Under this word start writing down as many one or two words that come to your mind. Think about the relationship you desire. What are the components of that relationship you want? What qualities do you think about? What does love mean to you? Write these words down. It will mean something different to each of us. So think about what it means to **you**. There will be times when you think you can't come up with any more words. Don't stop there. Keep going. Find at least 20 or more words to put down on your list.

Example:

LOVE

1. Happiness
2. Sees me as special
3. Suffocating
4. Fun
5. Adventurous
6. Willing
7. Playfulness
8. Friendship
9. Fulfillment
10. Excitement
11. Passionate
12. Unconditional
13. Creative
14. Trusting
15. Compassion
16. Thoughtful
17. Caring
18. Sacrifice
19. Sex

You get the picture… keep writing until you have at least 20 or more words on your paper. And here is something that is very important, when you think you can't find another word, find at least 2-3 more words. You will find that these last few words are indeed, the most important for you.

After getting all your words on paper, mark the ten that are the most important to you. These are what you want to have as beliefs about the word. Find the ten words that have the emotion of love for you. Which words resonate to you. You may have difficulty in choosing the words that you want to represent what you want for your love list. You can go back and rearrange them if you want to. Remember these are just beliefs and we can change our beliefs anytime we want to. Now rank them as to their importance to you, number one being the most important. Arrange them as to how you want to change your beliefs about the word. Put them in order of how you would like to think about love. If you would like to think about love meaning loyal as having more importance than fun, then put loyal as your number one belief.

If you don't like how you view love, this is where you change how you feel about it. If there are words or beliefs that you have in your list that you don't like, then take them out. And you certainly won't put them in your top ten will you? Becoming aware of what you think about a word allows you to change it. If you want to change how you view love, or any subject, take time to think about where these beliefs came from. Again, go into your past and find out how your parents, society, friends, family, media, view it. Then ask yourself, are these really how you want to view it? Or are you automatically putting them in your belief system without thinking.

Take time to ask your spirit how you would **LIKE** to believe about the subject. This is where the change occurs. By actually thinking about what *you* want to think about the word. If in your family, your father felt loved when your mother cooked dinner every night, and you find that you hate to cook, there might be some tensions in the love department. You might feel that you can not show love without cooking. Do you want to continue the familial pattern that cooking equates to love? Nothing wrong with this thought, but, you do not have to go along with what your parents or family passed down to you. Find out what gestures, thoughts or actions you do that shows your way of love.

If you come to an understanding that these thoughts and beliefs have come from how you were taught, change your belief to what you *want* to believe. This is when the liberation happens. You begin to come from your authentic self/spirit, not your memory and other peoples values. These beliefs will be yours. They were consciously chosen by you. These are how you relate to the world with your authentic voice. You have just chosen your belief system and you can change it at anytime. After all, beliefs are only beliefs and you can choose how you want to believe! Your belief becomes your destiny! Changing your beliefs changes your destiny, so take time in planning out how you want to live out your life.

Maybe you wrote down under your words for love, smothering. You might not have realized that you even had that thought. Maybe your relationship you are in now is smothering. (You will probably not want that in your top ten.) When you uncover your underlying belief system you will be more aware of what you have been choosing as a partner how you choose. A person who demonstrates a smothering type personality will no longer pique your interest. You will no longer equate it to love. If you have a relationship with this behavior of smothering, discuss it with your partner. See how you can come to some understanding with your partner that this trait is not one you consider loving anymore. Hopefully there will be a workable solution to help each other change some patterns to allow what each of you want to fulfill your love list. By changing your patterns, you evolve and are not compelled to repeat behaviors that keep you from having the love you want. We can change for the better when we become aware of how our thoughts dictate our behaviors.

Now look at your list for love. You might not be able to have all ten on your list, so pick out the top five. These top five are the deal breakers. Your top five are your *must haves* in a relationship you want. So, do take your time when selecting what is important to you. Not what you think it should be, but what you want it to be.

You can then use this list to help you find a relationship or alter your current one. If you are in a relationship that is not fulfilling, check and see if your top five are being met. If they are not, you may be in the wrong relationship, or you may want to work on these top five with your partner. There may be ways to change your communication or behaviors that will change your relationship to better fit your authentic self.

If you have not thought about what is that you find important for a relationship, you will not have the ingredients for a healthy, balanced relationship. Talk about this list with your partner. Communicate these needs that you have with your partner. If your partner does not know what your love list consists of, you are putting an unreasonable expectations on him or her. Your loved one knows nothing about how they might be able to realize your needs. This is unfair. You are expecting someone to fulfill your needs but they have to guess how to do that. Resentment can enter into a relationship when you do not know what your partner needs or wants. Take an afternoon or evening to do this fun exercise with your loved one. Or plan a romantic get away where this is something you will do as a couple.

Your "love list" may be different than your partners. You think that what is on your list is what most people want, or at least what your partner wants. You give to your partner what *you* actually want in the relationship. This may be the exact opposite of what is on their list. Without knowing what is on each others' love list you are creating unnecessary misunderstandings and conflict. Explain to your partner what it is that you consider love. Be clear to yourself first, what your underlying beliefs are.

One of your top five deal breakers may be that "love means spending every waking minute with your loved one." So, you go about finding ways to always be with them. Going on errands, being with them when they go out with their friends, being with them as they cook, clean or even taking a shower or bath. You think you are showing them love, because you are giving them the things that are on *your* top five list.

Now, if your partner needs time to be alone as one of their top five deal breakers, you can see how this relationship might collapse. You are trying to show how much you love them by spending every waking moment with them. Your partner feels smothered and trapped and will become angry and frustrated if they cannot get the time they need. You might become resentful because you think he/she does not appreciate your loving gestures. Your partner may try sneaking away or resorting to lying to you just to get the space they require to be happy and balanced.

This is an excellent exercise for both of you to do separately and then bring your list to the table. Share your lists with each other. Using your list, have an honest discussion about how you each are getting and giving what you want. Talk about ways you can bring more of each others lists, into the relationship. Communicating your top five with each other is fundamental in helping each other understand what love means to you. It takes away the need to mind read how the other person in your life views love. We each have our own belief system that may or may not be similar. Go find out yours and then communicate it to your loved one!

Understanding your communication style also helps in any relationship, whether it is a love, work relationship, friendship or family member. You may be an *inferential* or *ferential* type of communicator. My friend is an inferential communicator. She infers what she means, rather than tell me. She would come to my house and say something like "I am cold." Now, I am a ferential type communicator. I do not know what you want unless you tell me. So, when my inferential friend told me about being cold, I would probably say something like, you know I was cold the other day too. Or, it is suppose to get down to 40 degrees today.

An inferential type person is wanting you to know something without telling you. My friend probably wanted me to turn up the heat. I didn't understand that. So, she was hurt that I didn't do what she didn't ask me to do. She probably thinks I am insensitive.

My partner was also inferential. I once asked him what time it was. That is all I wanted to know. I was not inferring anything. I just wanted to know the time. He shot back at me that he was almost ready and to just calm down. He became irritated with me because he inferred that I wanted him to hurry up. Nope, I just wanted to know the time. Knowing your communication styles is important. It can help relieve undo hurts and help keep the arguments down. If your partner is ferential, you have to make sure you tell them what you want. Do not expect them to know.

Having an inferential partner means you will have to make sure you understand what it is that they want. By asking a direct question. If your partner asks if you are going to the store, or asks if there is milk in refrigerator, they may be asking you to go to the store to get milk. Ask them directly Do you want me to go to the store and get milk? Help them to tell you what they want rather than expect you to know.

Do this with any belief system you want to change. Try it on the words: money, career, family, relationships, sex, success, failure. Have fun experimenting with different words. You will begin to change your life when you begin to understand how you choose your life.

Here is a powerful true story that illustrates just how powerful your thoughts are and how they can influence your body.

Mr. Wright was a patient with advanced lymphoma, which had become resistant to all palliative treatments available at the time. Because he was anemic, his doctors did not attempt to use radiotherapy or the only chemotherapy agent available at that time, nitrogen mustard. The patient had "huge tumor masses, the size of oranges ... in the neck, groin, chest and abdomen. He was bedridden and dependent on oxygen; the only treatment that helped was a sedative. At the time, the American Medical Association was conducting a study into the usefulness of an alternative cancer remedy called krebiozen. The medical association had allocated enough drugs to treat 12 patients at the clinic where Mr. Wright was being treated. The study protocol specifically stipulated that patients would be considered for the study only if their life expectancy was at least three months. However, when Mr. Wright heard that krebiozen was available. He begged and pleaded to be put on the trial. Eventually against his own better judgment, his doctor, Dr Phillip West, agreed and gave him the first dose of krebiozen on a Friday. By the following Monday, Mr. Wright was a changed man. The tumor masses melted "like snowballs on a hot stove" and Mr. Wright "was walking around the ward, chatting happily, with the nurses, and spreading his message of good cheer to anyone who would listen. Kerbiozen seemed to work brilliantly, but only on one patient—Mr. Wright. In all other patients at the clinic there was no other responses, and within two months, all the other clinics in the study reported no successes. Hearing all this bad news Mr. Wright's faith waned, and after two months of near-perfect health, he relapsed to his original state. At this point, Dr West was the opportunity to double-check the efficacy of krebiozen. He deliberately lied to the patient and told him that the newspapers were wrong and that drug seemed to be working after all. He then told him that the relapse was caused by the drug's short shelf life—it had deteriorated while in the pharmacy. Then Dr West said that he had a new preparation of double-strength krebiozen that was due to arrive in two days. Two days later, with Mr. Wright in a state of eager anticipation Dr West started giving him injections of pure water. The results of the water injections were even more dramatic than with the original krebiozen. His condition went into another remission, which lasted for another two months. At that time, the American Medical Association made a final announcement that nationwide tests had shown krebiozen to be useless. Mr. Wright was now readmitted to the hospital, his faith gone, and his last hope vanished. He succumbed in less than two days.

Mr. Wright had believed in the success of this new drug, so he became healthy for two months and not just once, but twice.

Creating positive belief systems will produce magnificent events. Having negative belief systems can create tragic results. It is your choice on what you believe. It is up to you which way you direct your life and how you want to react to the events in your life. Your thoughts hold the power to your life.

6

A LOT OF TOOTHPICKS

Did you know that there are two million bits of information coming at us per second. The human brain can only process around 184 bits of information per second. There is so much information going on all around us at all times and we are only able to perceive just a teeny tiny bit of what is right in front of us. So, what does this actually mean? How can you use this information to help you?

Well, let's get a visual image first. Visualize a glass tube coming down from the ceiling in your living room all the way down to the floor. Now imagine that toothpicks are flowing down that tube at a rate of two million per second. That is a lot of toothpicks! Think about only being able to pull out 184 toothpicks out of those 2 million per second. As you can see there are a lot of toothpicks going down that tube that you are not pulling out.

Our brain is like that. There are so many things coming at us and we can only see/feel/comprehend only a minuscule of what is really going on. Our conscious mind is very limited in perceiving all of the information surrounding us. So, what is it that your mind pulls out? It pulls out only the bits and information that you believe in and are aware of.

What you pick out, are what *you* call <u>YOUR</u> reality. Those thoughts you yank out are going to be different than what your friend or children, pull out. There is so much more reality going on that you do not even realize. The 184 bits of information your friends pull out is what they consider *their* reality. We all do this. We take in information and say "this is the way it is". You think your perception is the only reality that exists. This is simply not so. Let me explain it this way. Suppose you just bought a red sports car. You will find yourself noticing more red cars on the road. Let's say you are pregnant, you begin to notice more pregnant women. You may think that there actually are more red cars and pregnant women, when in fact, there are the same amount. It is your awareness that is now focused on the red car or pregnancies. It is this focus that makes you think that there are more. Your attention is focused differently than another person. You are pulling out the toothpicks that say, red car or pregnant women because you are paying attention to what is on *your* mind. .Do you see how there is a difference of opinion in a given situation? Or that there are more than one way to perceive something? Other people are not noticing the red cars and pregnant women like you are. They might have just had an accident that day and now they are noticing all the accidents on the freeway, while you are seeing red cars and pregnant women.

The bits of information that you pull out depend entirely on what your belief system tells you. If you have a belief that people do not like you, then out of all of the information coming at you, you will only notice the thoughts that are aligned with your belief about people not liking you. You will not hear your co worker say what an awesome job they think you performed. Or, your friend telling you that you are thoughtful or kind.

What you will hear is that your co worker thought you were a bit weak in a part of your presentation. You think that what you just pulled out is the *only* truth in the situation, and you react to it that way, by saying things to yourself that you are not liked by anyone. You react to an illusion. You react to what you think is the whole truth. You think it is real and react to it as if it is real. It is not the only truth or reality. There are almost two million other ways to perceive that situation. Your way or your toothpicks are not the one and only reality. But you believe that it is. You believe that you are not worthy or likeable.

Do you want to change your reality about your negative self image? Then start looking for the other two million bits of information. Find those things that show that you are likeable and smart and are fine just the way you are. They are there, you just have to change your belief system to one that says you are wonderful, caring and a good loyal friend. What you have been doing is going into your memory bank and remembering all of the things that you have done in the past which resulted in what you consider failures or mistakes. This incident too, will go into your files under "I am a loser and no one likes me." You can see how the file grows.

Under your file of "I am wonderful," you will probably find it empty or at the very least only containing a few memories. That is because you never hear those wonderful things said about you. You are not even paying attention to those incidents. Those wonderful things you don't hear are the other two million toothpicks that pass you by. Your 184 toothpicks that you pick out are the same ones that are in your loser file. Your neural network is filled with them. Start filling up your wonderful files by paying attention to the information you have been ignoring. This is how you can start to do that.

Just by reading the above you now have a new way to understand yourself and what is happening to you. Yes, you have just made a new neuropathway. It is as easy as that. If you would like to continue making some more neural connections then continue reading!

Here is what you can do to add to your "I am wonderful" file. The first step you just took. You are understanding how things work. Now you need to be a bit more diligent in your hearing and feeling department. This will be like starting a new exercise routine. It will take some practice and you might be a bit clumsy at first, but if you are serious about jump starting yourself to a better you, a more joyous you, then do not give up. Now that you know your "file" on the wonderful you, pull it up in your mind. If you don't have on, make one. Envision that file, use your imagination and create what that file says on the label.

Throughout your day, notice what you hear, do or say. Pay attention to the wonderful things. Create times when you are the wonderful you. Think of things you can do, say or be, that will add pages to your "wonderful file". Show yourself that you have these qualities.

Do you smile at the clerk at the store? Help someone with heavy groceries? Tell someone how much you appreciate them? Small things may seem insignificant, but you will never know how you might change someone's day by letting them ahead of you on the freeway or saying a friendly hello to a stranger in need. These are the building blocks of that wonderful you that others will immediately feel. This changes the energy around you. Others will notice the difference also and begin to change their feelings towards you. You start to feel good about yourself and others will feel good about being in your company. Become aware of all the kindness in you and how you may demonstrate these acts to others.

These wonderful things are inside of you, they have always been there. If you can think of something wonderful and kind, then know that it came from inside of you. As you begin to do this exercise on a daily basis, memories will begin to float up to your awareness of times in the past that you have forgotten. You will begin to allow all of those memories of when you denied yourself the knowledge of being wonderful. Bring them into your life. Remember them. Think about them. Put them in your "file".

This is a new skill for you, but it is a powerful one that will change your life. You can do this with any part of your life where you feel you want to change. It doesn't have to be creating a "I am wonderful". It can be:

- I am successful

- I am attractive

- I know how to make money

- I am smart

- I am kind

- I am creative

- I am a great friend, parent, lover

You are creating a new file for yourself that has not been there before or has very few pages. You add to your file by finding the times when you *are* what you want to be. You will see and understand that you have those qualities you think you are lacking. It is just that you have not been noticing them and putting them in your memory bank.

We create our reality based on what our beliefs are. We then we pull that into our life and we call it real. We do not even think there is another reality. We believe it is the only reality, hook, line an sinker! You now know that you can create whatever reality you want.

We believe it because we prove to ourselves through what we hear and feel out of the 184 bits of information we bring into our world. When we keep pulling into our world what our belief system tells us, we continue to believe it is true. Your beliefs are not necessarily true. We only think they are. They are only beliefs you have been carrying around for years. We are not understanding that another almost 2 million bits of information bypass us each second. We create our reality by those tiny little 184 bits.

You automatically process your reality without all the "facts." What you experience is only the information that fills your belief of yourself. Your reality is limited. The good news is you can change what 184 bits you choose. You can learn to change your sense of reality and release yourself from the boundaries you created. You do that by changing your belief system. After all it is only a belief.

Beliefs are like fences around us. They separate us from all the other reality that is flowing down that tube. They can trap us in a prison and make us think that all the good stuff happens only to other people, not us. We are creating our own lives by what we believe. That's right! You create your own reality, and if you want your reality changed, change your beliefs. You get what you focus on. So, focus on what you want, not what you don't want.

Another example: If you focus on getting another job, you will pull into your reality the bits of information about new job openings and strategies on looking for a job or other careers that interest you. You will begin to see articles and interviews on how to go about putting your resume together for a better position. You will be talking about it and people in your life will know you are looking for a new job. They may know someone who can help you. There are so many ways in which you can find that new job. But, it first takes thinking about it. Your thoughts are your most important and powerful tool to create the life you want and deserve. Thoughts are a power tool.

Uncovering your beliefs and changing them to what YOU want is how you go about changing aspects of your life that are no longer working for you. There are no boundaries, only those you build yourself.

EXERCISE 5. LOOKING AT YOURSELF WITHOUT JUDGEMENT

Here is an exercise to help you understand and to get in touch with yourself without judgment or being attached to your belief system. Take whatever time you need to experience this. Read through it first and then take a few minutes to do the exercise.

Start *by letting yourself just experience whatever it is that you are feeling or thinking. Free yourself from all thoughts of right or wrong. Allow yourself to just be. Feel your breath as you breathe in and out. Feel what emotions arise and do not question if you are doing it correctly. Whatever feelings or emotions come up for you, feel them. Just feel them and be aware of them. Allow yourself to know that they are only thoughts. Accept them and be ok with them no matter what comes up. Be with whatever thoughts come up. Do not push thoughts away that may be unpleasant for you. Take a few moments to sense this and you will find yourself centered in your own being. This is you and your experience.*

Whatever experience you have in doing this exercise, will help you get in touch with yourself. Electromagnetic rhythms go out from you in all directions. This is the uniqueness of you. They are yours uniquely. Doing this exercise frequently will allow you to get acquainted with the inner you and allow you to accept your limitless reality and develop your communication with the "authentic" you.

7

FEAR

Fear keeps the human being from evolving. Can you imagine a life without fear? Or, better yet, an entire society? I am reminded of John Lennon's' song, Imagine, and I like to imagine what life would be like without fear? Can you?

First, let me say that there are two types of fear, *rational* and *irrational*. We do not want to get rid of the rational fear. It is hard wired into us. If we were walking in the woods and a bear came charging at us, it is rational to be afraid of that bear. It is rational to think quickly and figure out what to do. Do I run or fight? It would be foolish to not have this kind of fear. It is why you are here reading this now. You would not be alive if this type of fear were not a part of you. If you were not afraid to go swimming with the sharks or didn't run like crazy if someone twice your size was coming at you with malice in his eyes and a weapon in his hand, you would not have made it this far. That is why we have the fight or flight syndrome locked into our cellular core, to keep the human species alive! We have to figure out if we are going to run like crazy to get out of that situation or stay and fight it with whatever tools you might have. This type of fear is a good thing!

The fight or flight reaction is not the kind of fear I am talking about. This is called rational fear. It is the *irrational* fear that is not healthy for you. Our bodies take care of us and want us to survive. We have an *unconscious mind* that runs our body. It knows how to take care of you without you even thinking about it. It has the perfect blueprint for you on how to keep you perfectly healthy.

If you cut your arm, you do not have to think about what chemicals your brain needs to make to send to the open wound. Your unconscious mind does that for you. It takes care of healing you. If you get out of the way that is. So, before I begin to imagine a life with no fear, I will be talking about having no *irrational* fear.

Imagine no fear in your own life. Think what it would be like have no fear of public speaking, telling others of your views if they differ from theirs. Or what about having no fear of not being able to pay your bills or having to stand up to your boss that might be bullying you. To live in a state of knowing that you have the confidence in the universe and yourself that you will be able handle whatever comes into your life.

Imagine not being afraid of getting sick or breaking up with a loved one. Think about having the understanding that many things come into your life, things you may not like but know you have many necessary lessons and learnings that come with each experience. There is a reason for what happens, look within to find that reason. Your job is to find that reason.   Go on, keep imagining what it would be like to not have some of the fears you deal with daily.

Look at all the things we can be afraid of:

- Rejection

- Moving to a new home, town or country

- Getting physically hurt

- Being sick
- Changing jobs
- Getting caught in a lie
- Commitment
- Lack of commitment
- Being alone
- Being in love
- Not being in love
- Getting old
- People knowing who I am
- Homeless
- Death
- Loss of freedom
- Not being lovable
- Not being good enough
- Driving, flying
- Heights
- Water, swimming
- Ghosts, aliens
- Bad guys
- People
- Spiders
- Animals
- IRS

- Success

- Failure

- Leaving your house, being out in public (agoraphobia)

- Or, fear of *any* change at all

There are many more things people can be afraid of. I have not exhausted the list.

Now think about what it would be like to not be afraid of anything on your list. Imagine what you would do with your life if you had NO FEARS at all. What would you do? The things we could accomplish if we were not held back by our irrational fears. The peace that would come into our lives when the fear is gone. Wow! Pretty powerful living that would be. That is how many of us would love to live our lives.

The majority of our fears, come from irrational fears. Fear is the basis for diseases and illness in us. Just think what fear does to our body. A good example of this is PTSD. This is a common diagnosis used by many therapists to explain symptoms arising from a previous traumatic event that happened in the past. Some of the symptoms include:

- **Difficulty falling or staying asleep**

- **Irritability or outbursts of anger**

- **Difficulty concentrating**

- **Hypervigilance (on constant "red alert")**

- **Feeling jumpy and easily startled**

- **Anger and irritability**

- **Guilt, shame, or self-blame**

- **Substance abuse**

- **Depression and hopelessness**

- **Suicidal thoughts and feelings**

- **Feeling alienated and alone**

- **Feelings of mistrust and betrayal**

- **Headaches, stomach problems, chest pain**

As you can see, there are many physical and mental symptoms from this disorder. People suffering from PTSD have real symptoms than affect daily living and can cause a deterioration in their emotional and physical health.

What actually is causing PTSD? Thoughts! There is nothing harmful happening to the individual when the thoughts occur. Someone suffering with PTSD can be sitting in their living room, calmly talking with their family or friends, when a thought intrudes. This thought, will cause extreme distress, possibly even violence from the sufferer to another loved one or themselves. And understand, this is only a thought causing this.

Remember what happens with each thought we have? It creates a corresponding chemical. Thoughts are extremely powerful. They create our well being or discomfort.

A fearful thought creates a chemical that produces fear. It is not the other way around. Fear does not create the thought. The thought of fear comes first. The reaction comes *after* the "fear chemical" is released into your body.

Continual thoughts about the traumatic event leads to these PTSD symptoms. It is no longer the event that causes the distress in people with PTSD, it is the thoughts around the event. There is no pain happening, they are not experiencing the event, they are experiencing only the thoughts around the event.

It is the fear and the thoughts *of* the fear that brings about this debilitating disorder. If there were no fear thoughts surrounding the initial event, there would be no PTSD. Of course it is a normal reaction to fear being hurt physically or having any intense stressful incident.

Changing how you perceive that event, so that there is a meaning to the event, a learning from your spirit of why that has come into your life, changes the dynamics of healing this episode for you. You will no longer have to obsessively think about the event or feel hopeless or helpless. You will see how this event gave you insight and helped re-direct your life. You get your power back by looking at the event through your spiritual eyes. And seeing the event/situation as a way for you to learn something about yourself. When you can learn to change your thoughts around a traumatic event, it changes how you react to it.

The negative emotions surrounding irrational fear does not protect you. Holding on to this emotion is not in alignment with your spirit. Clinging on to this emotion is in direct conflict with your inner well being and health. There is no benefit from hanging on to a negative emotion. Learning what there is to learn from having this event in your life is better than preserving the emotions from the event.

I can speak of using this understanding personally. It happened while living in Costa Rica. We built a house that was far from other neighbors. We were surrounded acres and acres of rainforest. My partner had gone to the states to visit his elderly mother. I stayed at the house, alone.

About four days of being there alone at 3 a.m. two men broke through our safety bars in the kitchen and came into my bedroom and started to beat me with a bat. Being awakened in this vicious manner, I was not comprehending what was really happening. After screaming and wondering when I would awaken out of this nightmare, because this definitely was not really happening, these things only happen to other people, I heard my spirit guide tell me something. It told me is was no use screaming. No one could here me. There were no neighbors close enough that could hear anything from our house. Time slowed down for me as I had this conversation with spirit. It said that in 3 more breaths, I would allow myself to go into a deeply calm meditative state. I vividly remember how my adrenalin was pumping through my body and how my breaths were loud as I gasped for more air to scream for help. I recall counting down three, two, now on this next breath Robyn you will fall into this calm condition. I trusted this message but wondered how I could pull it off. "Ok, here goes" I told myself. On the third breath I easily went limp. I fell to the ground and the beating stopped.

The two robbers must have thought they had killed me as they felt for my pulse on my neck. I was not in an altered state, I allowed my body to calm down and I felt at peace. The two thieves went about tying me up and raped me and then went on with the carting out all of our stuff that they had their eyes on. I would sneak a peek at them as I wanted to be able to identify them if I survived this ordeal. But being pitch black I could only see glimpses of them as they held their flashlight in their mouths as they rummaged through our belongings. Peace was what I felt throughout this entire ordeal. I have a belief system that tells me that this is a safe universe, and that all things happen for reasons. And I was given the opportunity to put this "belief system" in practice. Lucky me!

When they found our gun, I thought I would have three options at this point. I would be shot and badly hurt or paralyzed, I would be killed or I would be ok. I found myself completely at peace and confident that I would handle what ever came my way with any of these scenarios.

Well, I am here writing this, so I was not killed or shot. They grabbed as much loot as possible and left. My badly battered and bruised body healed in the coming weeks. There was no permanent damage.

I actually found some humor in the situation. As I went into this peaceful place of meditation, the thieves, thinking they had just killed me, grabbed my necklace hanging around my neck. It was an inexpensive one, made with a beautiful seed strung on a leather string. They didn't take it. I was offended. "what?" I thought, "This is not good enough for you?" I was lucid for the entire event, at peace knowing that I would have the ability to face whatever was going to happen next.

In the next few days I began thinking about why this happened to me, what did I need to learn from having this in my life. I did not spend my time feeling sorry for myself or wondering what I could have done. I began to go deep inside to find the answers for what this lesson meant for me.

I do not suffer from PTSD. I do not mean to come across as arrogant or unfeeling, as I know there are many people suffering from trauma in their lives. I am suggesting that there are other ways to handle tragic situations. I think that when we look for our own answers from our spiritual side, we are not victims in life.

We are here to have experiences and to learn something from the experiences. It is up to us to come to our own understanding as to what messages, learnings or meaning the experience has for us. This helps us evolve and move on to the next lesson. Because, if we do not get the learning our being intends for us, we will get another opportunity to learn. And wouldn't it be better to learn the first time? I would not like to have another trauma filled event in my life to teach me this lesson if I can gently learn it by listening to my inner being in the first place. As I look back on this event of the attack on me, I can see how there were earlier, less disturbing events that were trying to get me to pay attention. There were many, as a matter of fact, that I ignored. I ignored them because I felt like I could power through each situation. I did not listen to what these situations might be wanting me to understand. So I ignored the signs and gentle tugging from my spirit to pay attention.

As I did not heed the lesson time after time, I gave myself a big wake-up call, so that I could not ignore the message I needed to move on in my life. The attack helped me to get "unstuck" in my life. I needed to update my purpose and this event helped me to do that. I feel like I had to be literally beaten over the head to stop and learn what was going to lead me in a different direction. That would not have been necessary if I would have taken the first hint.

Pay attention to the small voice you have inside you. Watch for patterns in your life that keep re-occurring. There is a message in there for you.

8

UNCONDITIONAL LOVE

Just as fear has different types, rational and irrational, love also has different types. The Greeks had four different words for love.

1. **Agape**-A deeper sense of "true love." Total love.

2. **Eros**- a passionate love, with sensual desire and longing.

3. **Philia**- friendship love. Loyalty to friends and family

4. **Storge**-affection as in affection for offspring.

I want to focus on Agape and Eros love. Of these two, we probably are more familiar with Eros love. Eros type of love is coming at us from every angle. Books, movies, songs, fairy tales, all are chock-full of the perfect love story. Finding, losing then finding again that one love and then being told that your life will become wonderful when you can possess that one person and have them love you. Think of all the movies with this as their main message:

- Gone With The Wind

- A Love Story

- Message in a Bottle

- The Notebook

- Pretty Woman

- Princess Bride

- Legends of the Fall

- Romeo and Juliet

I could go on and on with this list. It encompasses all types of people, rich and poor, young and old, smart and well, not so smart. It is not limited to time periods, from biblical times to modern times to future times. Nor are age groups limited. From Harold and Maude to On Golden Pond. Everyone gets the opportunity to look for and have this type of everlasting love. It is being touted as the one thing that will make you happy forever, if only you find that one true love.

We hear religions preach to the masses about how important it is to find love and get married. How many TV movies are about Eros love. We are bombarded daily from the time we are little to the day we die about how important it is for us to find happiness through Eros love. We are taught to continually seek and search for this one person so that we can be fulfilled and happy.

Look at the fairy tales we grew up with representing the Eros theme:

- Cinderella

- Snow White

- The Little Mermaid

- Sleeping Beauty

These fables are training us to believe that finding your one true love will result in your happiness forever and ever. It puts the focus on this enduring, sacrificing, long suffering love story. The heart of these stories is the challenge in finding and capturing your suitable mate. The longing for this person is what makes the story. These stories usually end when the two lovers finally agree to share their lives forever. This really is the beginning of a true love story, not the end. Eros love makes us believe the requirement to giving us a perfect fairy tale ending is for that one person to commit to you. Is finding your one true love the way to generate love in your life forever and ever? Let's keep looking.

Think about all the self help books teaching us how to keep this wonderful Eros love. Why do we need all these books and guidelines and seminars to help us keep this forever. I don't recall Cinderella or Snow White reading any of these books. What message are we missing in the fairy tale? If the characters in the movies and books stay together in love forever and they don't need marriage counseling why don't they tell us how to do this? They aren't telling the whole truth. Maybe there is a reason we want to believe these fairy tales as fact. What would be the purpose in that? It may be that it is just easier to find our fulfillment in another. There is a feeling of euphoria from Eros love. It mimics the feeling of being connected to universal love. As we search for feelings that make us complete and fulfilled, it is so much easier to grab the quick fix in a relationship of the Eros type. Our yearning for that "fairy tale" love is actually a yearning to get back to our connectedness with spirit.

How many people do you know in your life that have this type of relationship that allows each person to grow into the best person they can and is not about power or control struggles. A relationship that does not have one person submitting to the other. A relationship that does not pull you away from your individual path of evolution? While traditional relationships may have worked in the past, there is a thirst for a different type of relationship for many who want to stabilize their relationship with themselves first. Completeness cannot be found in another person. That is why so many relationships do not endure. You find euphoria in the other, and then one day wake up and still feel incomplete. You begin to be disappointed in your mate for not being the cure for completing you. Completeness comes from developing a connection to yourself which links you to unconditional love. A love of the entire universe. A love from the universe.

Eros love seems limited and maybe even a bit selfish. Eros love can die. It can go sideways. It can stop. Just look at the divorce rate. Some statistics state it is over 50%. Half of all marriages end in divorce. The percentage climbs for 2nd and 3rd marriages. This percentage rate isn't even accounting for live-in relationships. Many couples choose to stay in an unhappy, unfulfilling relationship. They may not be in the divorce statistics but could be categorized as still being unhappy and wanting something more or different in their lives. Even though their dream of a happily ever after has vanished, they may endure a marriage that is no longer promising them that happiness that was their hope in the beginning.

Usually after a breakup comes pain. Many experience a massive, deeply painful grief. It is the dread of "oh no! Wonder if that was my one and only person to whom I will ever be able to find happiness. Wonder if I never find another love again. What am I going to do with my life now?" The fear (irrational) of thinking that your one chance at finding that eternal bliss on earth just walked out the front door can be overwhelming. Overwhelming enough to stay in the relationship and suffer. The fear of living alone, maybe even dying alone can also be a reason to tolerate the relationship. A relationship may be the distraction keeping you from having to live your life to your potential. If that excuse is taken away from you, now what do you do? That is a scary prospect for some. When there is a break-up, it will be those same fears that sends you out searching again for another true love.

Let's take a look at Agape love. Agape means love for many. It has been written that it is the highest and purest form of love. It comes from your spirit, not your ego. It is a freer type of love demanding nothing in return. It doesn't go away. It does not die. It is forever. There are no restrictions and expectations coming from Agape love.

I have nothing against Eros love. It can be beautiful and rewarding and breathtaking to be in love. What I want to point out is that we as a society are not relating the importance of Agape love. Our children and youth are not being taught about the virtues of Agape love. Media, family, religion and friends have been teaching us that to find true happiness you need to find it through a love relationship (Eros). I would like it if these same sources would include the advantages of agape love as being just as important if not more important, in obtaining happiness and completeness as Eros love.

Agape is unconditional love. Unconditional love is loving with your soul, your inner being. Your inner being has no judgment. When you love unconditionally that means you love with no boundaries or conditions. This type of love comes from a place where there are no judgments. Your ego has a lot of judgment and conditions. Your spirit has none.

Your ego is the one who says I can only love someone if she thinks like me. Or if he makes as much money as me. They have to be of the same faith as me. She has to be blonde, brown or red hair. They can not be overweight, unhealthy, be unemployed. They have to be attractive, young, smart. Your ego is the one making the list for you on who you can love. There is nothing wrong with this list. But it is not coming from your divine source. Let's start teaching our children that Eros love is not the only thing to be on the lookout for when searching for fulfillment. Let's start teaching and learning how to love with our spirit.

Namaste is a beautiful word. I love this word. It translates into "the spirit in me, loves/respects the spirit in you." Wouldn't that be a wonderful place to be seen from? To have someone love you just for being you. Just for understanding that this life is not always easy and we make choices that we might have wished we had not. That we can be weak and vulnerable or stupid and cranky. Then someone comes along and tells us that the spirit inside of them understands all this and loves us anyway. And knows that you are on your path or journey in this life and you are exactly where you need to be and that is ok. And they love you anyway. And wherever you are on that path is just where you are and there is room to improve, but they love you anyway. Agape love has no judgments for anything you have done or are doing.

Someone loving with Agape love, just understands and knows that this is your life. They respect your journey and have compassion for whatever that leads you to. They want nothing from you. No demands that you act this way or that way. Everything is just fine the way it is and the way you are. You are a light being, a spiritual essence that deserves this unconditional love for your travels here on earth. After all, this life is just an illusion. Reality *is* this Agape love and reality exists in this Agape love. Being loved unconditionally helps you find your balance in this world.

Would that not be the most amazing kind of life to have. Having people in your life that loves you in this manner? Isn't that more of a healing kind of love? Unconditional love is more meaningful for us as a society, than Eros love. I think it is what the world is lacking. We see Agape love in action when tragedy strikes. Think of 9/11, Katrina, the tsunami in Indonesia. We saw Agape love at work. People were just loving and connecting and finding ways to help without judgment. It is in all of us all of the time. It is too bad that it takes a tragedy for it to be found. It would be wonderful if we could start sharing this type of love with those in our life and those who happen to pass through our life. Seeing a mother struggle with a crying baby in the market, instead of wishing she would get the child to stop screaming so you won't have to hear it, you could send this unconditional love to her and the baby. We don't know what her journey consists of. She could be abused by her husband at home. She could not have enough money to even buy formula or food for her family. With Agape love it doesn't matter. We honor her and send her this energy of non judgmental love for her just being here in front of you. You get the opportunity to send her healing love.

It would be great to see more movies built around a person who experiences this. To explore what a life like this would be like. To show how gratifying it is to live an ordinary or extraordinary life exuding this type of passion. There is enough room in this world for both types of love to be explored in the media and in real life.

Understand that having both types of love creates balance in your life. Having the choice of having both Eros and Agape love to come from, opens up your options to have a more inclusive way of being. If you want more of this in your life find ways to practice agape love. Next time you have a friend who calls you and is struggling through a difficult time, practice listening with Agape love. Don't tell this friend what to do, or how to think. Remember who you are, a light being full of Agape love. Practice being this light being by listening to your friend from this loving part of yourself. Listen to them with your heart. Talk to them with this part of your being. Agape love has no judgment for what you are hearing, it only has compassion. Let them know you are there for them and do not judge the situation. This is their journey in life, we are here to support them through this. Help those in your life find their way to their own answers. You can feel the difference when you talk with Agape love. You can see the difference in the person you are talking to. They can be themselves and do not have to spend any energy hiding in shame. When you give a person the safety of being their authentic self, warts and all, it is an expression of your unconditional love. Now go out into your world and find ways to practice this and put this loving energy into the world.

9

WHAT NOW

I had a difficult time deciding on the best way to end this book. How was I going to tie it all together? So I left the last chapter blank knowing that eventually the idea would come. Well, it did and rather than figuring out a way to finish the book I wanted a way to continue the thoughts that are within these pages. The intent of the book was to help free you from limiting beliefs and allow your spirit to direct the course of your life you were born to live.

We have looked at ways to do this and the blockages that get in the way to your authentic self. We have looked through both spiritual and scientific methods in which to understand how our body works to bring us health and well being. Now with your knowledge of how to come from your authentic self, it is time to bring that voice into your world. In your own unique way.

It may be a big movement like Ghandi brought to the world or small like the woman who brings sack lunches to the homeless in her neighborhood or making friends and visiting someone who is lonely. It does not matter as long as you are listening to what your self is telling you to do. It is time to change the world. You can feel it. Millions across the world feel it and are impatiently awaiting change. The only way for this change to happen is for us to make it happen. We are the ones responsible for raising the vibration of the planet. Waiting for government officials or leaders to lead us is only wasting time. They are not the ones to make these changes, it has to come from those who are listening to their inner guide. The *what now* is a key element in continuing what you have learned about yourself. It is a way to bring your information to consciousness into the world that you live.

Our world is like a jigsaw puzzle. We each have a piece to bring to the picture. We do not know what the picture looks like until each of us brings their piece. Your uniqueness makes the picture complete. If you have been feeling like you have been waiting for something to happen to help you bring your part, the time is now. Let's bring our pieces together into our world and see what the picture looks like.

You don't have to be a perfect human being to follow your spiritual self. So you can't use the excuse of "wait until I learn one more thing" before you feel comfortable enough to follow your authentic self. Remember, we are practicing all of the time. That is why it is called a spiritual *practice*. We practice until the day we leave this dimension.

I do not think anyone knows everything and there is always something for each of us to learn, or else there would be no reason for us to still be here. I don't even know what perfect is. Or, is there a perfect? Perfect is a value judgment using other peoples values. I interpret perfect as authentic. When you listen to your inner voice and act on that inner voice, this is what I call authentic. Perfection doesn't have a place in living a spiritual life. Our goal is not to be perfect, it is to be authentic.

I would also like to re define the word success. Success is finding your authentic self. Nothing more. It may sound simple, but in today's fast paced world the difficulty comes into play because we do not make a place for us to commune with our spiritual side of our life. Knowing our authentic self and then using that voice in everyday life is a spiritual practice. There are many, many ways to practice and it is up to each individual to decide how they want to practice. Practice means you get to practice this every day.

Success does not mean making a million dollars or having a private jet or being with the hottest looking partner. It is finding a way to live your life with your purpose. Find your authentic self and then be that in whatever way you interpret this to mean to you.

So now you are learning and practicing to be the authentic you and are feeling that there is something for you to do. You feel a yearning but you just don't know where to start. So many of us distract ourselves at this point rather than finding that place to start. We try to cut off these feelings that grow inside of us. There are millions of ways we distract ourselves. We watch TV, spend hours on the internet, shop, drink, sleep and eat. Each of these acts are not necessarily methods of distraction until you understand motive and intent for doing these things. When we are trying not to feel something we go into distraction mode. The uneasy feelings of being disconnected with community wells up and we have conveniently learned that by going shopping or finding something to eat or drink alleviates that emotion from arising. We have become disenfranchised from our families and our neighbors in this last century. Finding your way to reconnect to your surroundings adds positive emotional bonding and raises the vibration to whatever you are associated with.

We are only as healthy as our community ...our community is our planet. The need to re connect to our community/planet is the feeling of discontent we are trying not to feel. Many feel this undercurrent of disquiet and not sure what it is or what to do about it. One thing we can do is reconnect to people. It is so important that we find ways to connect to others and help our community. What I am proposing is taking time to feel that loss and then do something about it. Do not distract yourself from the feeling. Feel it. And then look inside for your unique way you can bring something to your community. You want a better environment for yourself and your loved ones? Be the catalyst to shift your world to what you want it to become.

There are many areas that face challenges and could benefit from positive energy you would bring. Let's look at some innovative people who are already bringing their uniqueness to their community. These people are visionary leaders who see a problem and then find a solution.

First off, let's meet Brenda Palmer Barber. She saw a problem in her community in Chicago. There was a 26% unemployment rate. She thinks it was much higher but 26% in any community is devastating. Many of these unemployed were ex-convicts unable to find jobs. She founded Sweet Beginnings. A company that makes skin care products from raw honey. And here is where her visionary skills came in to play, she hired ex cons. She gave them a place to begin to transform their lives by giving them her trust that they could be good, loyal employees. She looked past the stigma that our society gives ex cons and built a thriving lucrative business by training them to work with bees. She saw a problem and found a solution and not only assisted many people who before had no hope, she helped her community come together and become stronger.

Next up is Andy Lipkis. He founded TreePeople in Los Angeles. TreePeople focuses on promoting the creation of sustainable urban ecosystems through education and the planting and care of trees. But it is sooo much more than that. Andy has a love of trees that began when he was 15 and spent time in the mountains of Southern California. He is responsible for planting a million trees in time for the Olympics in 1984. He organized a tree planting project for Martin Luther King Blvd. where 500 trees were planted in honor of Mr. Kings birth date. Which turned into a living monument to Dr. King. This went far beyond the tree planting for people who were involved in this project. They said it changed their lives. Many participants had never been a part of a community action project. They got a true sense of being a part of helping their community. Andy has many accomplishments with his TreePeople and one I would like to share with you is his work in the Los Angeles school district. He looked at the budget for improving the schools and noticed that half the budget was for re-paving the schoolyard with asphalt. A sum of 187 million dollars was going to pave the land in this watershed. The budget also called for putting in air conditioning units. Andy felt that no one had linked the blacktop and lack of trees with the need for air conditioning. There was resistance to planting trees rather than using asphalt. Andy was able to show how the schools could actually have the trees pay for themselves and actually save money and also save energy. He was able to provide both the greening of schools and provide education for the students that are monitoring the progress of the trees. He is changing the landscape of his community and helps in providing jobs and creating a place where people can come together to work towards a sustainable future. In his own words, Andy describes the act of involving yourself like this, "When you see pain and need, it's easiest to shut it down and turn away by saying that I don't have to feel that or respond to that because there is nothing I can do about it. But when you allow yourself to become involved you have to pay attention and respond. It doesn't take extraordinary talents or resources to achieve miracles. So much of the learning and the power comes from just getting on a path and doing it."

I am not saying that each of us have to do something awe inspiring like these two individuals. Find something that you can bring your uniqueness to. Look around your world, what things do you see that could work better, be different or changed. Be aware of your surroundings and take time to discover what feelings are stirred. Do you see social problems in your life that bring up emotions for you? Follow those thoughts and feelings. Imagine what it might take to change that into something better. Be curious.

It doesn't take the entire world to help change something. It only takes a tribe. Find your tribe. A tribe is a social group. Seth Godin in his book Tribes states that "...lasting and substantive change can be best effected by a tribe, a group of people connected to each other, to a leader and to an idea." You can join a tribe by finding something you are interested in and becoming a part of that. Or you can start your own tribe by finding people who care about your idea or project.

There are many areas that need changing. I am giving but a few suggestions here, please let your creativity add to this list. Many social problems in our world are centered around:

- Poverty

- Homelessness

- Hunger

- Safety

- Crime

- Health

- Education

- Unemployment

- Abuse: drug,/alcohol/ sexual/ physical

- Sustainable living

- Healthy food

- Isolation

For each category listed above there are many solutions. Become a part of the solution. Come together for solutions by forming think tanks, activism, cross cultural dialogue to lift us to new ideas. We need curious teachers and leaders and students to inspire change.

Take what you are learning about yourself and put it into your world. Find a way to shift charity into an enterprise and create a few jobs for others. New philosophies are necessary to visualize concepts toward fixing Humpty Dumpty. Think outside of the box and do not succumb to thinking that nothing can be done or that you can't change it. It is more important to be putting those positive feelings into your environment than actually changing the situation. It is the feelings and emotions put towards the project that actually do the change. Your *feelings* of caring and empathy is what is necessary to facilitate change. Feelings of love and caring raise the vibration of those around you and lifts us up to the next level. With this love and concern we will change our planet.

Understand your uniqueness and wonder how you can use that uniqueness to alter something in your world. Just like Andy Lipkis took his love of trees and found a way to give his gift of what he loves to our world. If you are interested in organic food, give a class at your community center on the benefits of eating organic. Start a weekly outing by bringing people to a farmers market. Or teach a class on cooking organically. Find ways to create community. It is this community that will raise the vibration of the nation.

If your neighborhood has a homeless population (which city doesn't) collect food, clothing, blankets or toiletries and bring them to a shelter. Encourage others to participate using your emotions that you feel. Talk to them about what it is that you are feeling towards your project. Express your feelings and they will feel it also.

Experiments show that feelings and emotions in the heart change DNA. We can heal our bodies and our world through creating feelings of care, appreciation, gratitude – these emotions trigger healing. When people were asked "What is the shift?" at a recent conference where scientists and speakers for scientific study gathered, they all said basically the same thing. That we are in a critical time period and must learn to transform our thoughts to effect the healing of the earth. .

The old way of thinking was that it took "x" number of people to achieve change. Science is learning that it is not about the number of people but about the quality of the inner experience of the people. A miracle is only a miracle until we understand how it is performed and then it becomes a technology that we can apply again and again. We are still learning and we don't yet have all the answers but we have learned the that the power of human emotion heals and we can put that to use now.

I want to leave you with this example of the power of emotion. We have two satellites that are above North America which send signals back every 30 minutes showing us the strength of the magnetic fields of the earth. On 9/11 those readings went off the chart. This was the first time that scientists learned that the human emotion of millions of people watching their television sets that day and feeling those emotions of what happened on 9/11, was so great that it actually spiked the magnetic fields of the earth. This magnetic field is what connects us all and links all life. What it told us is, we have the ability to influence the very fields that connect all things and all people. We accomplish this by connecting to others with love and compassion. This is how we can change the world. This is how we will change the world.

I ask the question, "Do we need another 911 tragedy to bring us together in love or do we want to start changing our world today by transforming ourselves into beings who see the world in a new way. You can start to change your world by choosing to see others as beings of light who are living their life the best they can. And by seeing others with compassion. Perceive events and situations as opportunities to learn something about yourself. Put your unique gifts to use and those gifts will change the electromagnetic field around you, your loved ones and your community and our world.

The world is waiting for you.

EXERCISES

EXERCISE 1. <u>LOOKING FOR YOUR PURPOSE</u> (Chapter 2)

When looking for your purpose use these questions to help you with your search. Write the answers to these questions in your journal. Take time to answer these questions with thoughtfulness.

1. What makes you smile? (Activities, people, events, hobbies, projects, etc.)

2. What were your favorite things to do in the past? What about now?

3. What activities make you lose track of time?

4. What makes you feel great about yourself?

5. Who inspires you most? (Anyone you know or do not know. Family, friends, authors, artists, leaders, etc.) Which qualities inspire you, in each person?

6. What are you naturally good at? (Skills, abilities, gifts etc.)

7. What do people typically ask you for help in?

8. If you had to teach something, what would you teach?

9. What would you regret not fully doing, being or having in your life?

10. You are now 90 years old, sitting on a rocking chair outside your porch; you can feel the spring breeze gently brushing against your face. You are blissful and happy, and are pleased with the wonderful life you've been blessed with. Looking back at your life and all that you've achieved and acquired, all the relationships you've developed; what matters to you most? List them out.

11. What are your deepest values?

12. What were some challenges, difficulties and hardships you've overcome or are in the process of overcoming? How did you do it?

13. What causes do you strongly believe in? Connect with?

14. If you could get a message across to a large group of people. Who would those people be? What would your message be?

15. Given your talents, passions and values. How could you use these resources to serve, to help, to contribute? (to people, beings, causes, organization, environment, planet, etc.)

EXERCISE 2. <u>5 QUESTIONS</u> (Chapter 2)

1. "Who Am I?" What kind of person are you? What's been true of you since you were younger? Write down all the attributes that you can think of that are truly you. List the things you naturally have learned and developed over the years. You probably take these things for granted, not recognizing them for the special, significant and unique gifts they actually are.

2. "What Do I Love To Do?" What do you absolutely, truly enjoy doing in your professional life? In your personal

life? For each answer, consider the gifts that have helped make them possible. Your purpose will involve doing something that you love.

3. "What Experiences In Life Were Really Fulfilling For Me?" Look for the times in your life that were fulfilling for you. These were times when you were just being yourself. Consider, What was it like for me while I was going through it? What was I feeling? What was important, special or meaningful for me? These answers hold the key to what you should be doing with your life.

4. "What Am I Afraid Of?" Once you know what your purpose in life is, what will keep you from living it? Fear is the number one thing that stops people from being who they were meant to be. Do you want to be fulfilled? Then feel the fear, and do it anyway.

5. "How Do I Put My Purpose In Place?" Your life is moving forward whether you are working towards your purpose or not. So, wouldn't it be better to take one action each day that will get you closer to who you were meant to be? It could be as simple as making a phone call, sending an email, or doing some research on the Internet. Your purpose will be realized one step at a time until one day you find that you are living it. And what if you've done all this work and it hasn't come to you yet? It will. We were all put here for a reason. And, if you are determined to find your purpose, it will come your way. When something that strong is in your heart, it's only a matter of time before you discover what it is. The answer is out there; it's just a matter of finding the right question.

EXERCISE 3. FOCUS ON YOUR AUTHENTIC SELF (Chapter 3)

Let's do an exercise to help you practice focusing on the authentic self. Take a moment to not only read this but actually do the exercise. Read through the next paragraph first then come back and do the exercise. It is very simple and doesn't take much energy or thinking to do.

Stop and take a breath… A long deep slow breath…While doing this relax the muscles in your body and around your eyes….. okay, take one more long, slow, relaxing breath. And just relax and let any thoughts come up. Do not try and focus on any one thought, just allow any and all thoughts to come any way they want. Again keep relaxing and take three more breaths…..

Okay, now that you have done this little experiment answer these questions.

Did you feel the difference of what you felt before you took the breaths? How about after you took your breaths? What were your thoughts? What were you thinking or saying to yourself? Did your "mind chatter" continue? Does it slow down? Are you thinking about all the stuff you have to do, or did you envision something calm and peaceful. Learning to stop and allow your thoughts come up is the beginning steps to learn how to communicate with your higher self. It is time to get in touch with this part of yourself that you have been neglecting for many years. You may not have even been introduced to this part of you yet. Your higher self, authentic self , inner self, or spiritual self or any other word that works for you has been waiting for you to listen.

EXERCISE 4. <u>CHANGING YOUR BELIEFS</u> (Chapter 5)

Ok, so let's see what is required to go on a hunt for those repressed beliefs. How *do* we find our belief system? Good question. And there are numerous ways to go about this very important task. Here is one way that has helped many of my clients.

First of all pick a word or belief that you want to find more about. A word or a belief that you want to see where your ideas around it came from. For instance take the word LOVE…. Lots of different ways to view that word. All of us have our own way we think about it. Let's take a look and see what your belief system is, about love.

Write the word *love* at the top of a piece of paper. Under this word start writing down as many one or two words that come to your mind. Think about the relationship you desire, what are the components of that relationship you want. What qualities do you think about. What does love mean to you. Write these words down. It will mean something different to others. So think about what it means to you. There will be times when you think you can't come up with any more words. Don't stop there. Keep going. Find at least 20 or more words to put down on your list.

Example:

<u>LOVE</u>

1. Happiness

2. Sees me as special

3. Suffocating

4. Fun

5. Adventurous

6. Willing

7. Playfulness

8. Friendship

9. Fulfillment

10. Excitement

11. Passionate

12. Passionate

13. Unconditional

14. Creative

15. Trusting

16. Compassion

17. Thoughtful

18. Caring

19. Sacrifice

20. Sex

You get the picture... keep writing until you have at least 20 or more words on your paper. And here is something that is very important. When you think you can't find another word, find at least 2-3 more words. You will find that these last few words are indeed, the most important for you.

After getting all your words on paper, mark the ten that are the most important to you. These are what you want to have as beliefs about the word. Find the ten words that have the emotion of love for you. Which words resonate to you. You may have difficulty in choosing the words that you want to represent what you want for your love list. You can go back and rearrange them if you want to. Remember these are just beliefs and we can change our beliefs anytime we want to. Now rank them as to their importance to you, number one being the most important. Arrange them as to how you want to change your beliefs about the word. Put them in order of how you would like to think about love. If you would like to think about love meaning loyal as having more importance than fun, then put loyal as your number one belief.

If you don't like how you view love, this is where you change how you feel about it. If there are words or beliefs that you have in your list that you don't like, then take them out. And you certainly won't put them in your top ten will you? Becoming aware of what you think about a word allows you to change it. If you want to change how you view love, or any subject, take time to think about where these beliefs came from. Again, go into your past with your family and find out how your parents, society, friends, family, media, view it? And then ask yourself, are these really how you want to view it? Or are you automatically putting them in your belief system without thinking.

Take time to ask your spirit how you would **LIKE** to believe about the subject. This is where the change occurs.

If you come to an understanding that these thoughts and beliefs have come from how you were taught, not how you may think you change your belief to what you want to believe.

EXERCISE 5. <u>LOOKING AT YOURSELF WITHOUT JUDGEMENT</u> (Chapter 7)

Here is an exercise to help you understand and to get in touch with yourself without judgment or being attached to your belief system. Take whatever time you need to experience this. Read through it first and then take a few minutes to do the exercise.

Start *by letting yourself just experience whatever it is that you are feeling or thinking. Free yourself from all thoughts of right or wrong. Allow yourself to just be. Feel your breath as you breathe in and out. Feel what emotions arise and do not question if you are doing it correctly. Whatever feelings or emotions come up for you, feel them. Just feel them and be aware of them. Allow yourself to know that they are only thoughts. Accept them and be ok with them no matter what comes up. Be with whatever thoughts come up. Do not push thoughts away that may be unpleasant for you. Take a few moments to sense this and you will find yourself centered in your own being. This is you and your experience.*

Whatever experience you have doing this exercise will help you get in touch with yourself. Electromagnetic rhythms go out from you in all directions. This is the uniqueness of you. They are yours uniquely. Doing this exercise frequently will allow you to get acquainted with the inner you and allow you to accept your limitless reality and develop your communication with the authentic you.